CARVING OUT A CULINARY CAREER

Chef Evelyn Shelton, MPA

CARVING OUT A CULINARY CAREER

The Good, the Bad, and the Not-so-bright Decisions Made on My Jagged Journey to Restaurant Ownership

Chef Evelyn Shelton, MPA

Copyright ©2025 Evelyn Shelton, MPA

ISBN 979-8-9999098-0-0

All rights reserved. Printed in the United States. No part of this publication may be reproduced, transmitted in any form or by any means, electronic or mechanical, including photocopying, recording, or any other information retrieval system, without the written permission of the publisher, except by a reviewer who may quote brief passages or reproduce illustrations in a review with the appropriate credits.

This book is not intended to be a manual, guide or how-to resource. It is an account of the author's real-life experiences and cannot be used for the rendering of professional advice or services to the individual reader. Neither the author nor publisher shall be liable for any loss or damage allegedly arising from any information or suggestion in this book, as the ideas, procedures and suggestions included are not intended as a substitute for consulting a licensed professional.

>   Shelton, Evelyn
>
>   *Carving Out a Culinary Career*
>
>   Nonfiction/Business/Leadership

Notice: This book is not intended to act as an authority on legal or financial matters. It is recommended that you seek qualified professional assistance as a means of handling and caring for your business matters.

To my mom, Jessie Neal, my forever chef

Table of Contents

Foreword 1

Introduction 3

Part One: The Build Up

Chapter 1: How It All Began 13

Chapter 2: Franchise Or Culinary School 19

Chapter 3: Slow Start & Then 27

Chapter 4: Financing Dreams 33

Chapter 5: Beware Of Contractor Pyramid Schemes 43

Part Two: The Come Up

Chapter 6: Let The Floodgates Open 49

Chapter 7: Opportunities For Exposure 55

Chapter 8: Poppin' Up At Pop-Ups 67

Chapter 9: Global Pandemic, Big Opportunity 75

Chapter 10: When The Dotted Line Becomes A Lifeline 79

Part Three: The Breakthrough

Chapter 11: Mo' Business, Mo' Money 87

Chapter 12: Business Enterprise Program (BEP) Certification 95

Chapter 13: Nourishing Folks Using State Contracts 99

Chapter 14: Mind Your Taxes & Your Accountant 105

Chapter 15: The Business Of Acquiring Grants 109

Chapter 16: Consumer Packaged Goods (CPG) 115
Conclusion 119
Resources 129
Review 131
About the Author 133

Foreword

Kimberly Wells, former executive producer and fill-in host Operation Breadbasket presents 'Harambee!'

"How-to" books and manuals exist for a reason—mostly to guide the reader from one point to the next while teaching them the necessary steps to do or to become something. This book isn't that. Instead, *Carving out a Culinary Career* is the important and real story of the key ingredients required of small business owners such as listening to yourself, having faith in your dreams and abilities, planning and following through—and yes, making ample mistakes. These are the "secret sauces" that have allowed Chef Evelyn to forge her own way, to create her own path, and to embark on her own journey to restaurant ownership. Here, she candidly and vividly portrays wit, wisdom, and a wry look at what it costs to be the boss. This book will both inspire and motivate you to bet on yourself and believe you can win.

With her blueprint—often funny, but always honest—Chef Evelyn holds nothing back on the journey of how she prepared, paid her dues, and did what was necessary to shape her culinary vision. With proven culinary skills and backed by reputable credentials, she took a chance on herself. And with a willingness to lay it all bare she presents her journey here to aid those who desire to do the same. This is her next gamble. She is betting on you, the reader, to glean something from her past—the good, bad and ugly of it all. It is a unique opportunity to not do what she did on her path but to arm yourself on your own path.

There is much you can learn from the successes of others, perhaps more from their missteps. Chef Evelyn masterfully paves the way with stories and examples of how each breadcrumb, laden with clues, can aid in the development of your own business roadmap. That is, if a culinary career is what you desire, or if becoming a restaurateur is in your heart, and growing beyond restaurant ownership is on your bucket list.

Let Chef Evelyn's years of experience and belief in herself (and her team) be the necessary north star for your entrepreneurial efforts. *Carving out a Culinary Career* is a Chicago story, no doubt, but a story that will resonate with many in the food industry—fans and critics alike. Chef Evelyn's tale is easily relatable anywhere in the world because the desire to provide amazing food and to be successful at it can be found in every corner of the globe. However, her journey—one that starts at home—is indeed still evolving with you in mind.

May this be your next best step to your own journey ahead. Carving Out a Culinary Career is a feast, so devour. Dine sufficiently and let it nourish all of your aspirations.

Introduction

I recall eagerly attending the National Restaurant Association show at McCormick Place in Chicago, in May of 2016. Chef Vivian Howard, one of my favorite celebrity chefs, would be speaking, so I arrived early enough to get a good seat. I was especially excited to hear her story in her own words.

The room was packed, and Chef Vivian was engaging, funny, and honest about her culinary journey. Her transparency moved me in such a way that I listened to her with great intention. She had moved from North Carolina to attend the Institute of Culinary Education in New York City, and she shared her experience with running her own restaurants and suffering the devastating loss of one due to a fire soon after the start of her PBS series, "A Chef's Life." Listening to her felt exciting to me; she was interesting as well as informative. I later had an opportunity to ask her advice for those of us also aspiring to open our own restaurant.

Chef Vivian's hilarious answer was short, to the point, and perhaps a cautionary warning that I should have heeded: "DON'T!" She then laughed for several seconds, amusing herself as much as she amused the audience before going on to say that she was mostly kidding since she very much enjoyed her experiences as a restaurateur. What I did not know at the time was—one year later, in May of 2017—I would open my own establishment, Evelyn's Food Love. And a little less than three years later, I would have a second space in one of the food halls in that very same venue where I spoke with Chef Vivian:

McCormick Place, the largest convention center in North America.

Since opening my restaurant, many aspiring chefs or restaurant owners have called or stopped by asking me the same question I asked Chef Vivian and several more. Questions like how I opened my restaurant, how I navigated the pandemic, how I acquire contracts and grants, and what I wish I'd known prior to opening. I am always happy to answer any question about my personal journey, and I do so frequently enough that a friend suggested I put it all in writing. And that's what you are holding—the tangible manifestation of a foodie turned chef, corporate chef turned entrepreneur.

Being a chef can be difficult, to say the least. Being a Black chef in a corporate environment can be nearly impossible. Being a Black female chef in a corporate environment is a rarity that brings with it its own unique challenges. I would be remiss in not acknowledging any would-be entrepreneur whenever and wherever they reach out. This project is done with the intent for some budding business owner to benefit from hearing my story, particularly if that entrepreneur is contemplating opening a small restaurant or café.

Given my experience, I am especially invested in small restaurants or cafés that may operate in disinvested communities. However, this is *not* a self-help book nor a how-to on restaurant ownership. *Carving out a Culinary Career* is for the entrepreneur who is willing to put in the work; do the heavy lifting. It is not for the person who has abundant resources or all the answers, which is the complete opposite of my experience.

What I am going to outline here are the steps I took to open my restaurant on the South Side of Chicago—the same South Side that is seemingly always portrayed in the most negative light in the media, both locally and nationally. I will share the good, the bad, and the not-so-bright decisions I made along the way. This story will unfold authentically. I am including everything there is to know about my "jagged journey." After all, when people witness the final product, they often may not appreciate the sacrifices made, or perhaps inaccurately assume that the journey is linear or easy. Far from it!

Instead, I am sharing the knowledge I wish was imparted to me before I embarked upon my journey. I heavily advise against learning as you go when entering the Hospitality industry as an independent owner/operator. Well, not unless you just feel the need to be perpetually on the verge of losing your ever-loving mind, as I was close to on more than one occasion. If that's your goal, well then, have at it!

For simplicity, I will use the words "we" and "our" frequently, even though I had no actual or legal business partners. In essence, I will be referring to my staff both past and present because I could not have done any of this without any of them. It truly does take a village to raise a child—and to run a successful business. Evelyn's Food Love, as I have also learned, needed a sound village of sound-minded people, as well as a mountain of resources to push past the rough patches.

I should emphasize here that without substantial and ongoing assistance, mostly financial, opening a restaurant is not an easy task. However, it is also not an impossible task, as evidenced by my journey. You will encounter plenty of naysayers, so try your hardest not to be distracted, dismayed, or deterred by them—no matter how loud – and trust me, they will be loud. The world will be hard enough on you, so give yourself grace and don't do the world any favors by being equally hard on yourself. Find your village or create one, and there will be enough supporters to come together—hopefully, with ample encouragement to drown out the negativity and to give you the confidence you will need to be successful, especially if you decide to go it alone.

Again, I do not necessarily recommend going it alone. I, however, had little choice or the choices I did have were not as appealing. And being a tad bit stubborn, on occasion—I did not want to defer my dreams because others could not see the vision quite as plainly as I could. There were hard lessons to learn, yet I yielded to the process and prevailed. *Carving out a Culinary Career* represents the abbreviated version of the highs and lows of my personal experiences.

In most situations, with few exceptions, I prefer succinct information—the Cliff Notes, or bullet points, if you will. That is what you have here. My preference is to thoroughly research just enough detail to prevent me from overthinking or talking myself out of something that might be the simplest and most rewarding option. Particularly if my self-doubt is based on fear induced by information overload. For me, something either makes sense, or it does not. I am typically quite comfortable making decisions and sometimes making mistakes based on whether something makes sense. This is my method—the "jagged journey." And it has worked for me (for the most part). And now, you get to use this resource, avoiding some of my mistakes, and make it work for you (for the most part).

To be honest, I have enjoyed a few shining moments and some seriously lackluster ones, too. And to be clear, I have made more than my share of mistakes prior to, during, and since opening Evelyn's Food Love—one or two of which could have proven catastrophic. Still, I will shamelessly share those mistakes. And, despite a series of unforeseen events—specifically, a global pandemic and living in a sanctuary city that, at one point, was inundated with migrants arriving daily—I successfully navigated and gained a deeper understanding of the business I am still passionate about nearly nine years after choosing to open a restaurant.

Although I did not have a personal mentor, I highly recommend you having one, two, or as many as you believe you may need. I had to figure out quite a bit on my own, and having a mentor might have made this part of my journey less jagged. Just like I sought out Chef Vivian Howard at the restaurant show in 2016 at the McCormick Place event, I invite you to find and follow someone who feeds your entrepreneurial spirit and who also delivers results in their own life. Until you connect with someone who can help guide you in a real and meaningful way, do not shy away from exploring other options—like, attending events, watching podcasts, or using social media posts, reels, and live videos. A mentor is a mentor, even if they don't know you are their mentee!

PART ONE

The Build Up

Now faith is the substance of things hoped for, the evidence of things not seen.

Hebrews 11:1 KJV

Chapter 1

How It All Began

Surprisingly, I began this journey equipped with a small business loan that was backed by the Small Business Administration (SBA), personal savings, credit cards with high limits and zero balances, and an excellent credit score. I was not familiar with their processes but quickly learned that the SBA does not actually lend money. They back loans should the small business default. So, I still had to find a lender and meet their specific qualifications before being approved for a loan that, again, the SBA would then back. One might presume this would potentially make qualified entrepreneurs more desirable applicants. However, that is not necessarily the case. At least not where traditional banks are concerned; and certainly not in my case.

I eventually found a non-traditional lender after getting my feelings thoroughly and completely stomped on by several traditional bankers who all but pointed and laughed when I inquired about financing for my business. However, after talking to one sympathetic banker, who enlightened me about the world of alternative lenders, I ended up with a cozy, yet trendy restaurant in an underserved community on Chicago's South Side. Before we get into that, my story actually began several years prior while I was still working in Corporate America.

At that time, I constantly prepared and took food to work for lunch and for staff meetings to share with coworkers. I enjoyed cooking and still often do it for nothing other than the immediate gratification of seeing the sheer joy on another's face after (or while) they enjoy a delicious meal or treat prepared by yours truly. Moi! The compliments I received provided just the right amount of incentive for me to keep the meals coming. I was told by one of my college professors in undergraduate school that the thing you don't mind doing for free is likely the thing you should be doing for a living. That way work will never really feel like work and when you do what you truly love, the money will surely come. She was so right.

My professor's words resonated with me at a time when I was searching for more, still trying to figure out a viable career path, yet still undecided. What she said made perfect sense and her words remained lodged somewhere in the back of my mind for many years. The thing I often did for free was cook. If someone was having an event—be it a birthday, a graduation, a simple movie night or whatever—I would volunteer to bring food. Someone sick? No worries. I would be right over with homemade soup and a platter of freshly baked cookies. One good friend swore my chicken noodle soup cured her cold within hours and that kind of gratuitous flattery was certainly good for my ego and ensuring more food in her future.

Things really started to change when people began offering to pay me to cook or cater events for them. It was exciting! Cooking for free was one thing, but preparing food that was good enough for people to offer me money? Well, that spoke volumes and was worthy of thorough entrepreneurial consideration.

Although free food generally tastes amazing and will also garner many compliments, I thought compliments certainly were not enough to open an entire restaurant – certainly can't pay any bills with compliments. Still, with that bit of inspiration, I began catering on the side and built a solid clientele. It was motivating, and some evenings and on most weekends I found myself putting together menus and meals for small gatherings of 10-40 people, which I could pull off with proper prep and minimal assistance. I made enough money from catering part-time to start socking away cash in a real business account and to ponder a culinary career a bit more seriously.

Although Corporate America continued to pay the bills, buy the house, and allowed me to raise and support my child, I did not waver from my goal of restaurant ownership. My corporate gig provided the comfort and stability we needed to live, I admit. However, having my job as my private investor made me comfortable, maybe a little too comfortable.

While I did not love my corporate job, I also didn't hate it. I was simply really good at it, so I was in no rush to leave. That was the conundrum. At the time, it did not matter that I knew absolutely for certain I would be far more content if I could just while away the days in my own kitchen, cooking and creating for others.

I also had no real plan, so I stayed squarely put in my comfort zone and remained there comfortably for several more years. I would say that I wasted a good deal of time, except that I am a firm believer in everything happening exactly when it is supposed to and this venture was no exception.

*****

I will say one of the biggest challenges I experienced early on was getting people to share information. Later I concluded that information is not regularly shared within certain circles for a reason—one being there are seemingly very few resources and opportunities available amongst minority entrepreneurs particularly in Hospitality. Therefore, when some of those rare opportunities surface, people can be closed mouth and circumspect until they have secured resources for themselves. I saw this quite a bit with grants, for example, specifically those with a limited number of awards. Why increase your own competition might be the thinking.

Quite frankly, I don't mind sharing information.

It is another reason why you're holding this book.

I truly believe, and without the slightest equivocation, that what is for me is coming directly to me. I offer you this resource in that spirit. I did not have a sense of community starting out. Still, I believe that if I am not fortunate enough to reap a certain benefit, then I want a woman or a person of color to have an equal chance at the same opportunity. This is how I feel, as there are seemingly endless platforms for non-minorities readily available.

"Leap, and the net will appear."

Les Brown

Chapter 2

Franchise Or Culinary School

I somehow always knew I would one day own a restaurant. I love good food; both of my parents grew up on farms in the south and both were scratch cooks. It was preordained.

I had been toying with the idea of restaurant ownership since my early twenties, and there was never a thought that it would not happen. It would, I just had no idea how or when. In my young mind, "how" and "when" were very minor details.

I fancied a bluesy, jazzy space with live music, amazing food and libation served to a classy crowd that didn't mind long waits or dropping a bill or two to enjoy the right vibe. That would not be the case, initially. In fact, it was almost the complete opposite. I started with a dilapidated building that previously housed a beauty salon and rehabbed it. The construction crew and I might have even stumbled upon an illegal juke joint in the basement, judging by the number of liquor bottles and old sofas we discarded.

****

Eventually, I would indeed leave the comforts of corporate. I started taking a series of free classes and educational workshops through the city's department of Business Affairs and Consumer Protection (BACP) to learn about licensing, inspections, and the basics of owning and operating a business in Chicago.

I also began researching franchise opportunities and was *closerthanthis* to purchasing a local chicken business. It was well known locally, starting to expand nationally, and had a profitable business model. It was a proven concept having been around for decades, and I even had familial connections through a previous marriage. However, more importantly, there was a great deal of flexibility, and the franchise fee was relatively modest compared to those of other national chains that were popular.

In frequenting several of the business locations, with the exception of the chicken, all of the owners appeared to be doing their own version of the same thing. I reasoned that I could sell the franchise's products and include my own signature side dishes, perhaps adding homemade desserts to the menu. After building up a large and loyal following, I would strategically exit the franchise and rename the business. I was ready to play it safe but had no name in mind back then for the business I was contemplating opening. Later, I would elicit much help to settle on a name for my restaurant. Purchasing a franchise, however, was my initial, non-fleeting thought.

While mulling over the idea of the chicken franchise, a different franchise opportunity presented with a popular East Coast Caribbean concept looking to expand into the Chicago market. After some research, it seemed there was a considerable number of slightly disgruntled franchisees, so I opted out. While

I thoroughly considered both options, I was also actively looking into culinary schools at the behest of a dear friend.

There were several prominent schools in Chicago at the time, including one affiliated with The Art Institute of Chicago and another connected to Le Cordon Bleu. My friend and I debated the pros and cons of both options: purchase a franchise or attend culinary school. I obviously decided the latter would offer more suitable options—that and the cost of investing in a culinary education was a little less costly than the initial start-up fees associated with purchasing either of the franchises I was considering.

Although there were a few well-known culinary schools in Chicago, at the time, most have since folded. The school I attended, Kendall College, is still open and later became affiliated with National Louis University.

I weighed my choices carefully and the investment in a top culinary education would end up being the best option for me. After all, names really do open doors!

I admit as a seasoned cook and caterer prior to attending culinary school, I was not completely convinced that I would learn a great deal. I could not have been more wrong. I was thrilled to be enrolled in an accelerated program at a top school, taking culinary classes during the day and baking and pastry classes at night to fill my electives. The dean had shared with me that several students would attempt to complete both programs simultaneously each semester, but very few finished. *This sounded like a challenge!*

That narrative ended up being far more than a challenge because I often slept in my car between classes to stay focused. Going home between classes would almost guarantee distractions—mostly deep and meaningful sleep—that would all but ensure my lack of success.

And so much for any doubts I may have initially harbored. I learned so much after the first week of classes that I found it hard to imagine what I could possibly be learning a year later. Classes were so interesting that I only missed two days during the entire 15-month program. President Obama's motorcade caused one absence, and I will mention this to him whenever we meet. I don't recall the second instance, maybe I went home between classes.

By this time, I was fully immersed in my culinary experience. The aroma of red wine cooking at 6:00 a.m. became the norm and red wine cooking at any time of day still conjures up pleasant memories even today. The wine and food pairing class that I was not originally interested in became one of my favorite courses. I mean, who doesn't want a reason to eat good food and "taste" fine wines early on a Saturday morning? A little éméché at 9:00 a.m.? Yes, please! No matter how often the instructor insisted we simply "slosh" the wine around in our mouths and then discard it, the words seemed to fall on deaf ears. We sipped more than we sloshed - for the culinary culture! Nonetheless, this course would prove invaluable later, especially after we received our liquor licenses at the restaurant. But I knew back then that my future restaurant would eventually be in excellent hands: Mine.

Fifteen months later, I only needed a couple of additional pastry classes to receive the baking and pastry certificate that otherwise would have cost north of $10,000 had I enrolled in the program separately.

Upon completing both programs, I was off to start my *shiny* new career in the culinary industry with my *shiny* new degree and my *shiny* new certificate in hand. I nearly broke down in tears when most job offers came in at just above minimum wage. The offers were nowhere near what I had earned in my cushy corporate gig, not even in the ballpark. Far, far outside of the ballpark… Like, beyond the bleachers and the cheapest of the cheap seats.

What the hell had I done?

Had I put everything on the line for minimum wage and at least thirty grand in student loan debt? Significant student loan debt that I had never really had before because the cushy corporate gig provided a substantial amount of tuition reimbursement for both my undergrad and graduate degrees as a perk.

I felt physically ill. How did culinary school cost so much while netting so little opportunity at the end of the program? I mean, really? Law school costs a fortune but after passing the bar, you are a lawyer for Pete's sake. Medical school was slightly different though, kind of like culinary school, I reasoned. There were still internships and residencies to complete prior to becoming an attending physician, right? Long hours and poor pay when you added it all up happened before the real payoff….

I had to tell myself something, right? This worked.

I would be fine; it would just take a little time… Right?

"The only place where success comes before work is in the dictionary."

Vidal Sassoon

Chapter 3

Slow Start & Then

I was venting to one of my culinary instructors after class one evening, regarding the paltry career opportunities when he suggested I explore opportunities in corporate culinary since I already had a corporate background. This made sense. He then shared that working in restaurants could be great, particularly if you have youth on your side and years of work experience ahead of you. (Was he alluding to my age while trying not to directly allude to my age? Should I have been offended?)

Attempting to blow off what might have been reason to be offended I was serving some serious side eye before he added that the ability to feed the masses, as in corporate culinary, could net far bigger bucks and garner a better quality of life with evenings, weekends and holidays off. It was as compelling an argument as it was appealing, so I was inclined to forgive his earlier slight.

He further suggested that I put my new pastry skills to work immediately and sell desserts in my free time to keep up my baking skills while making money. He added that, in his experience, most people would buy desserts before they would purchase a meal. Something I had not considered since I am not big on sweets. He also pointed out that more people could afford to pay for pastries than could afford to pay for a fancy catered event, and he was right—for the most part. For several years, I was able to make ends meet (and then some) by selling mostly desserts and catered food items. I put together a simple website showcasing mostly pictures where I sold my modest but elegant wedding cakes and fancy desserts, offering creative and interesting catering menus as well.

My team and I kept busy with ideas like artisanal cheeses, breads and spreads that we made from scratch and handmade chocolate truffles. We once catered a wedding reception with hundreds of assorted hand-made truffles during a blizzard. And an Asian-themed birthday party for a 90-year-old guest of honor, complete with an elegant buffet table and two, cooked-to-order action stations. I have not made or eaten a truffle since then.

After about a year, I began looking for corporate positions. With my background, culinary credentials and other degrees, I began receiving much better offers within a few weeks. I landed at a small behavioral health hospital and revamped their entire food service program, including recipes and menus for staff, patients and events. This was less than a year prior to me being recruited back to the hospital where I had spent most of my corporate career. The food service director happened to remember me and hired me on the spot when I interviewed.

Within months after accepting her offer, I was taking my first "black box" culinary exam to become her executive chef—the first Black female executive chef at that account, a major medical center and a major feat. The "black box" included an assortment of raw ingredients in a box, all of which had to be used to create an appetizer, an entrée and sometimes dessert courses—no menus, recipes or instructions.

The "black box" test was designed to determine the ability, as well as the creativity, of the executive chef candidate. It also included a written exam of 30-40 culinary-related questions including menu costing, food cost percentages, and the latest food trends, most of which I learned while in culinary school.

I aced the exam once I got a firm grip on my nerves. A good friend, who literally walked me to the test site—which felt to me like the equivalent of walking the culinary "green mile"—saw how nervous I was. She literally elbowed me and yelled, "Snap out of it! This is what you do!"

That jolted me out of my trance, and I stayed in that role for more than a couple of years.

I worked in a few other corporate chef positions after that and before gaining experience as a food service director. It was then that I began putting together the pieces of my business plan in a cohesive manner. I kept copious notes as I gained front-of-the-house and back-of-the-house skills and experience in every position. Opening my own restaurant was now very much on the front burner.

"Start where you are. Use what you have.
Do what you can."
Tennis great, Arthur Ashe

Chapter 4

Financing Dreams

I began the process of restaurant ownership by writing a compelling narrative about my vision for the restaurant, the community in which it would exist, detailed menus, and my experience in the industry. It was comprehensive, and I would often tweak it for various grants and other business applications. Since numbers are not my strongest suit, I enlisted the help of an accountant to aid me with the financial projections once I completed the initial numbers and I included those projections in my five-year business plan. I was now several years post culinary school with extensive professional cooking and operations experience. I had learned a great deal and had also helped my previous employers meet their financial goals, it was now time to move on and increase my own finances. It was time to pray, step out on faith, and bet on me.

My next step was to talk to potential partners. One individual wanted to be a silent partner; all potential partners wanted to find, open, and operate a location in downtown Chicago. However, there were several problems with this, the main one being that I had long wanted to open my business in *my own* community—if not, at least somewhere on the South Side. Being a part of the solution by operating in an underserved community that could benefit from an economic boost was quite appealing to me. Surely other businesses would see my success and follow suit, right?

Well, not exactly.

At least not immediately.

I also began looking at properties that I might be able to purchase rather than lease, as real estate is a solid investment opportunity. I firmly believed if the business did not perform well, despite my best efforts, I would have a commercial property to rent or sell to recoup my investment and pay off any related debt. This would certainly be preferable to walking away with nothing, which was entirely possible if I invested all of my money in someone else's property and if I was willing to fund someone else's dream.

My potential investors wanted no part of my altruistic plans to save the South Side. Either I would open downtown where they believed we could see a reasonable return on our investments and reasonably quickly, or I would open without them and their semi-deep pockets. Ultimately, I followed my instincts—which I questioned many times—and moved forward with my original plans. I later realized it was the best decision I could have ever made.

It is important to note two things here. First, when I initially opened my business, I continued to work full-time as a food service director. I had accrued months of paid time off and used the flexibility to get the restaurant open. Plus, I needed the money and the benefits. I had a good amount of debt, and my credit cards were nearly maxed. The restaurant also could not yet support my salary. Additionally, I wanted to make sure I was investing in my staff so they would buy into the promise of the business. So, I continued to work because it clearly was not the time to burn any bridges or ships ala Hernán Cortés, quite frankly. Second, and most importantly, I did the one thing I promised myself I would never do: I used my home as collateral on a loan to open my business, a business that was certainly not as valuable as my home.

I generally consider myself a reasonably intelligent person, but this was clearly not one of my shining moments. Some may argue, this was not smart at all. I needed a place to live whether my business succeeded or not. So, theoretically, my home should have stayed off limits, and it did for many years. As it turned out, though, I would not have been able to get my business off the ground any other way since my plan was to own the property. Traditional banks were not willing to lend to a start-up. No matter how much experience I had, no matter how much education I had, neither I nor my restaurant were proven or bankable concepts yet.

Tragically, traditional banks had no interest in my dreams and far less interest in my heartfelt promises. I was starting to believe I would have fared far better had I purchased a franchise or opened downtown with investors. It wasn't until I called a small neighborhood Black-owned bank that I spoke to a small business manager in commercial lending, who broke it all down for me. She also provided some direction—no money but valuable, free insight and information.

I had no idea that getting even an SBA loan might prove to be a challenge. She referred me to several non-traditional business lenders and a couple of places where I could get free information and business coaching, such as the Chicago Urban League and the Service Core of Retired Executives (SCORE), which is an agency that works through the SBA. This was free information that was not only useful but eventually led to even more information.

Because I had limited funds and an unproven concept, I had no choice except the non-traditional lending route, which made collateral a requirement. This is typically the dilemma for many small business start-ups, specifically in minority communities—no access to capital, no access to collateral. This could be a significant barrier to acquiring SBA-backed loans as well, though there are a few agencies that do not always require collateral, like Allies for Community Business (A4CB), particularly if certain other requirements are met. Like it or not, I had collateral in the form of my home, and if I wanted to open my restaurant and to see an even larger return on the investment I'd made in a culinary education, then I would have to use the resource available. This inevitably put my home at risk and created a reasonable level of stress.

Fortunately, while applying for a loan, I did not have to worry about the presence of massive student loan debt that would prevent many small, minority-owned businesses from accessing loans. I had no undergrad or graduate school debt because of the corporate tuition reimbursement perk I had previously enjoyed; a lender could not count that against me. However, my culinary degree cost more than my graduate degree, and a small portion of that debt remained.

Using my home as collateral was risky, but I absolutely believe in the power of prayer—which I did regularly and sometimes loudly and publicly—and I believed in myself and my ability to make this work. Never mind the fact that I had never even worked in a restaurant. (That is, unless you count the fine dining, dining room in culinary school where I "worked" for one semester as a course requirement). I thought, *but really, how hard can it be to open and operate a small restaurant? Cook the food, serve the food, and collect the money, right?* I chuckle now at my naïveté. But there is power in being a little naïve, sort of in the same sense that ignorance is bliss. I did not overthink it, and I kept moving forward. *"Cook the food, serve the food, and collect the money,"* played on a loop in my head some days.

And so, I stepped out on faith.

I bet on myself and used my home as collateral to finance my dream. Yet with the unforeseen circumstance of a global pandemic looming less than a few years later, the risk of losing both my business and my home, in one fell swoop, would become a very real reality. I should have opened downtown in the warm embrace of those long-gone business partners, right? I was feeling much more than a little regret…or anxiety…I was feeling both, actually….

I would eventually spend personal savings and use personal credit cards, intentionally making minimal payments each month, to purchase day-to-day food and supplies to keep the restaurant open. My credit took a huge hit, as the amount of interest that accrued on large balances was insane, and my credit score dipped considerably and regularly. I began questioning the good sense God gave me.

A business associate, who would invest several thousand dollars on food and supplies prior to the restaurant opening—likely out of sheer pity—never once asked me for the money or otherwise put any pressure on me to repay the loan. Don't misunderstand… The restaurant was doing okay; it just needed to do better if I was to ever quit my day job and get a handle on the mountain of debt. But even when the pandemic hit, my business associate never said a word. Either she was the very epitome of a "silent partner," or again, it was pure pity. I'm pretty certain it was the latter.

That kind of debt remained in the front of my mind, and I prioritized repaying it while losing quite enough sleep most nights. Another friend (the same one who elbowed me prior to my first black box exam) wrote me a check for several thousand dollars as an emergency backup. I held onto that check for more than a year before hitting a very rough patch at the start of the pandemic. I almost cashed the check just after but decided to wait in case the worst was still to come. What if the pandemic proved to be even more problematic for my business long-term? At that point, everything was still left to be seen.

Although I was working mostly as an independent entrepreneur, I was blessed to have friends and other entities willing to contribute to my success. There was no way I would take advantage of that or let them down without putting forth significant effort.

Other than my friends, one entity that contributed regularly to my success was my lender. That's right, my lender became a partner of sorts and deeply invested in seeing me succeed. I am certain they did much of what they did not only to ensure my success, but to also ensure their repayment—a somewhat novel idea but perhaps one that should be replicated by other financial institutions, particularly those reluctant to lend to small businesses with yet-to-be-proven concepts.

When the restaurant became more profitable sometime later, the same bank that initially turned me down for a loan would later offer huge loans and business credit line opportunities. Evelyn's Food Love was now doing what they and other traditional banks had essentially said could not be done (presumably the reasons they would not invest): Create demand and in an underserved community.

*****

Evelyn's Food Love opened in May of 2017 after securing a mortgage on the property the previous year. I was referred to Local Initiatives Support Corporation (LISC) by a lender that was unable to provide the amount I would need to comfortably get the project off the ground.

LISC was not only able to help, but their stated mission was to assist small, minority, veteran, and woman-owned businesses in underserved communities. Boy, was I in luck! Except for veteran status, I was basically their mission statement incarnate.

How could they say no?

Well, because, I was told, they had not previously structured a loan to include property acquisition and rehab, they almost did say no. Still, "no" doesn't always mean, "no." Sometimes, "no" just means to try another way.

So, I would not relent. I kept reminding them of their mission statement to help bolster my case. They eventually agreed to fund my project and, honestly, the process was not simple. But I needed something from them; therefore, I had to tough it out. Their money, their rules. This would be an SBA-backed loan, so there were even more rules but with benefits I would not realize until years later during COVID.

I would indeed get the loan.

And dreams do indeed come true.

Prior to opening the restaurant, I would post information, videos and food pictures on social media. I enlisted friends to help me with naming the restaurant, picking signage, choosing logos… *Everything*. I was creating a following even before opening and gave them buy-in by openly asking for their input for the business.

They felt invested. I felt supported.

I felt seen. They felt heard.

Furthermore, I invited my social media friends over to eat, as my staff and I tested recipes prior to opening. I'd also invite them whenever media outlets were filming segments in the restaurant. This created even more buy-in, along with more buzz, and additional support.

"If you really want to do something, you'll find a way. If you don't, you'll find an excuse."

-*Jim Rohn*

Chapter 5

Beware Of Contractor Pyramid Schemes

When I eventually closed the loan and got the keys to my place it was time to hire an architect and a general contractor. Work went on for months, led by what must have been the worst general contractor known to man.

Because I have a real knack for choosing poorly at times, I often enlist help from people who are *much* smarter than me. I give myself plenty of credit, however, for understanding and embracing my limitations—and for reaching out to those whose strengths are my weakness. I have zero shame when I need help and there is no such thing as embarrassment when asking for said help is required. So, I surround myself with enough people who know what they are doing and lean on them when I need to.

The general contractor dragged my project out two months longer than necessary. He played what I can only describe as some kind of construction project pyramid game—a pyramid scheme for contractors. Beware of anyone who uses your money to fund their current project while praying for their next project to fund your project and so forth and so on. I would primarily recommend you start by getting plenty of recent references and checking their

Better Business Bureau (BBB) status prior to committing. Secondly, be sure to have your general contractor sign a contract reviewed by your attorney and not simply their own—a contract that includes a "time is of the essence" clause to protect your time, interests, and budget. Only pay a third of the fees up front, a third halfway through and the balance upon completion.

This "pyramid" scheme set off a chain of events that caused the general contractor to go over budget and lose subcontractors, while also pushing our opening back more than three months, costing me plenty. I was still happy I had not yet quit my day job and was able to continue bringing in a regular paycheck to meet the new expenses associated with the restaurant and this scheme. I had begun repaying the loan long before the first meal had been cooked, let alone served, and they were messing up both my time and my money. Subsequently, I replayed every decision I had made leading up to that point, again questioning my own sanity, wisdom, *or both* in the process. There I was a full-grown woman who wanted to call my big brother to come and have a man-to-man with this contractor. I didn't know what exactly that looked like, but I was not opposed to a slightly physical discussion. I felt wronged by the general contractor trying to take advantage of me likely because I am a woman. I eventually fired him and worked directly with the lender and the subcontractors to complete the project and to get the subcontractors paid.

Our soft opening finally occurred on a beautiful and warm spring evening in late May. The place was packed! Since the windows were covered during construction, it was unclear to the community what type of business was being established.

However, the signage had been recently delivered and installed: *Evelyn's Food Love*. I'm sure the name may have offered a clue.

There was very little fanfare when the restaurant was fully opened, and we experienced an unsettlingly slow start. I quickly learned that "likes" on social media absolutely do not translate into butts in seats or sales.

Fortunately, I had planned for it to be several months before people knew the restaurant even existed, and my staff and I plugged along. While there was a bit of a financial cushion in the bank, we were keenly aware that we needed more visibility. I wished for more business, more customers, and a bit more notoriety. I needed a marketing plan but had zero marketing dollars.

Once again, my non-traditional lender (LISC) came to the rescue and arranged for a marketing expert and for a professional photographer to write an article and snap pics for an article about the restaurant. That same writer shared my story with several high-profile media outlets, and all of them began doing the same.

Within a few months, the restaurant, staff and I were featured in several newspaper articles, magazines, online media outlets including Forbes, and on a few radio programs, including one national syndication out of New York. After each new interview another would follow and that did translate into more business; and plenty of butts in seats. I was also invited to speak as an expert on various panels. I did my fair share of getting our information out also.

PART TWO

The Come Up

Chapter 6

Let The Floodgates Open

There was a popular food segment that aired every Friday on one of the local news stations in Chicago called "The Hungry Hound." I reached out directly to the reporter several times inviting him to come by, enjoy a meal, and give us a few minutes on his news segment—our "15 minutes of fame," so to speak.

The host did not immediately respond, but I am not easily deterred.

I hounded The Hungry Hound until he answered. At the time, he said he was traveling somewhere in Asia and promised to reach out upon his return to the U.S. And after a couple of weeks, I began reaching out again.

One afternoon, while working my corporate gig, I was on the telephone with my chef manager, who was at the restaurant. She said abruptly, "I gotta go. Someone just came in and he doesn't look like a regular." She called me back several minutes later very excited saying, "It's the guy from Channel 7 News! It's him; he's here!" I told her to calm down and to make sure everything was perfect. I then instructed her to call me again after he left…

But I wasn't calm either.

I was actually pacing.

In that instant, I wanted to rush right over to the restaurant. However, I trusted my staff. They knew how to handle Evelyn's Food Love. And as with the gentleness and consistency of a good pot of properly simmered greens, they always hit the spot. "The Hungry Hound" was in more than capable hands, and I knew this because friends often called to compliment my staff on days they had visited the restaurant in my absence. This proved the ideal time to let my team know I trusted them implicitly with my "baby."

Still, when my corporate chef manager overheard my end of the conversation (and saw me pacing) he asked, "Would you like me to casually go by there and keep an eye on things?" I could not say "yes" quickly enough. He was an amazing cook, calm under pressure, and as capable as I am—if not more. He headed for the restaurant, and within what seemed like minutes, I got another call from my chef manager at the restaurant. She was calling back to say the reporter was "full, satisfied, and very complimentary of the food and the space." She reported that he was still there, kicked back and reading his newspaper. I thought about emailing him to see how he enjoyed his meal. Instead, I decided to give it a day or two before reaching out.

A few hours later, I received an email from the reporter indicating that he wanted to return with his film crew to shoot a segment for his show! He and I set the date for a month or so later and, yes, I invited those same social media friends who had been such a big part of my pre-opening process for a pleasant "surprise," suggesting they "dress to impress" for the occasion. In reality, I only told a handful of people what the real deal was. And, on the day of the taping, Evelyn's Food Love was packed with people who came to enjoy good food, live music and loads of fun—unawares!

The event also featured desserts from two of the dessert vendors we supported. My team put out some of our best and most popular menu items, then spruced up the dining room and kitchen. We'd only been open for a few months, so the place still felt new, and we enjoyed breaking it in. Still, I went all out hiring a professional cleaning crew so every "nook and cranny" would be ready for close ups, capturing the walls that were painted in warm colors with a deep red ceiling, exposed brick, and wood floors.

The taping was hugely successful! The team and I were invited to go to the studio on the day the segment would air a few weeks later. We took several of our most popular dishes with us and watched in-studio with the rest of Chicago. We could not even imagine the onslaught that was about to become our reality for the next several months. This is what I'd wished for, more visibility. And to that I would only caution, be careful what you wish for because you just might get it!

*****

As my management team and I were leaving the television studio after the segment aired, the production manager smiled and said, "Let the floodgates open!" We all chuckled, and at about the same time, all of our phones began blowing up. Vibrations and ringtones galore!

The team at the restaurant was calling to say the phones were ringing off the hooks, the place was packed, and they were running out of food! My managers left the studio heading for the restaurant while my chef manager and I headed to the restaurant supply store. By the time he and I made it back to the restaurant, the place was still packed, and one cook was in the backyard smoking a cigarette and crying some serious tears. She was explaining between sobs, "We were not ready for this." The chef calmly said, "So, this is your solution? C'mon. Let's get to work. This is what we wanted, right? Vacation is over." Then chef looked at me, winked and grinned. I smiled and nodded.

And so, it began.

Months of more business than we ever knew was even possible.

I vividly remember the first time I went shopping after that segment aired. It was then that I realized I didn't have to charge the $2,000 bill for the food and supplies piled up in my cart because there was finally ample and extra cash in the bank. What an amazing feeling that was!

I had an inkling, at that point, that with just a few minor adjustments, we could really make this a successful venture. And we were not even downtown! I knew, from personal experience, that Chicagoans will travel for good food—no matter the location. I recall standing in line, regularly, for some of the best BBQ in the city in a restaurant located right across the street from Cabrini Green where cult classic Cooley High was filmed—one of the most notorious housing projects in the country at the time—without the slightest regard for personal safety. Good food will do that. Good food will make you risk life and limb for a taste of something amazing.

I noted to myself that my staff and I would need to capitalize on the moment to extend our 15 minutes of fame. I was sure the momentum was finite because customers were coming from all over the state to check us out after "The Hungry Hound" sniffed us out—with a little "bone-dangling" encouragement from me. Some people were even coming from out of town. We quickly determined these new faces were likely not our regular customer base and we knew we needed to keep the main thing the main thing: Good food. We simply needed to stay focused, enjoy the moment, and get paid for the duration—however long the duration lasted.

"The Hungry Hound" episode that originally aired was supposed to only air once, maybe twice, that Friday. It ended up airing all weekend long, several times between Friday and Sunday. It was explosive! Customers were pulling up to Evelyn's Food Love in taxis, some were coming directly from Midway Airport—a straight shot from the restaurant. The segment was so successful that it ran across screens in the back of taxicabs! It was pure insanity—in the best possible way.

My staff would open the shades, most mornings, well before we opened for business. And to our sheer surprise the lines would already be forming. Customers would enter and ask, "Do you know that your line is way down the street?!" *Down the street?*

Due to the popularity, we found ourselves closing the restaurant two days each week instead of one. We needed an additional day just to shop and prep for the other five days of service. The cooks were preparing everything from scratch, getting fresh produce from an urban farm a couple of blocks away from the restaurant, and changing up our menus often. They were doing all of this as well as making the seasonings and rubs that I had been perfecting for years while working in corporate, and quietly using those customers as my test subjects.

That one television appearance would be the first of many media appearances, including radio, newspapers, magazines and more—both locally and a few nationally. It was great for business and allowed us to enjoy a steady stream of customers and other opportunities, like catering, pop-ups, festivals and various other food events.

Chapter 7

Opportunities For Exposure

When the phone rang, I was in the office. The restaurant was fairly busy, and the caller ID read, "McCormick Place." Since McCormick Place is the largest convention center in North America and located in Chicago, I answered without hesitation. I even wondered if they had dialed the wrong number.

I had no idea why McCormick Place would be contacting us, but I am always as excited as I am open to a challenge or an opportunity. When I answered, the person on the other end introduced himself as the vice president of SAVOR Chicago. This was the company managing the food service operations at the facility at the time. He indicated that he had gotten my information from someone whose name wasn't familiar to me, but who I later learned was an executive at the Metropolitan Pier and Exposition Authority that manages Navy Pier and McCormick Place in Chicago. She had gotten my name from someone at our lending agency. (Yes, LISC came through yet again!)

The vice president on the other end of the receiver shared that SAVOR was interested in a partnership with Evelyn's Food Love where we might provide products to be sold at the convention center in one of their existing restaurants, cafes, or shops. I had motioned to my chef manger to pick up the extension, as I knew it was always a good idea to have another set of ears listening just in case I missed something in the excitement. This was, after all, McCormick Place— did I say the largest convention center in North America? Surely, this would be a great opportunity and hopefully a very profitable one as well. The restaurant had been open for less than two years, so this was an exciting next step that we were eager to explore.

As we both listened intently, the vice president went on to explain how we might provide a product and earn a percentage based on sales. By the end of the conversation, he was scheduled to visit the restaurant with a team member within a few days. This gave us a couple of days to strategize and strategize, we did.

When the SAVOR team arrived a few days later, my chef manager began serving one amazing dish after another—all of which had been seasoned with our unique rubs and seasonings, while I explained the dishes. I suggested our guests pace themselves since the plan was for them to taste quite a few items and let them know the cooks would gladly box anything they could not finish. We had no idea what a collaboration could or would look like so our strategy was to simply throw as many delicious dishes and food ideas as we could at this opportunity. We sought to make it hard for them to decide, and it worked.

My chef manager and I watched as the SAVOR crew ate, smiled, and asked questions, analyzing what they were tasting. They spoke between themselves and began to explain that they had a space inside of their food court that they were planning to refresh. Then they asked if I would be interested in having a version of Evelyn's Food Love operate in the food court at McCormick Place. *Was I!* I was cool and composed on the outside, but on the inside, I was beyond ecstatic. I was already thanking God and calculating potential revenue in my head.

I answered, very calmly, "That sounds interesting. I'd like to learn more." I then asked precisely how would this work. My chef manager and I were invited to stop by a few days later, to look at the space, and to continue the discussion. Within a few days we were at McCormick Place, looking at the space that Evelyn's Food Love would soon occupy.

This all seemed so very exciting. We discussed what SAVOR Chicago was interested in, which was a menu of no more than six or so items. Apparently, during large conventions, the more precise the menus, the easier it is for customers to choose and keep long lines moving.

The SAVOR team was interested in our dry rubbed catfish, chicken, baby back ribs, collard greens, black-eyed peas, and hush puppies. But to replicate what we were doing in the restaurant, at McCormick Place, my team and I would have to re-create the recipes for large volume, and SAVOR would have to purchase the rubs directly from us. *Boom! Another potential revenue stream.*

When they agreed and sent over the contract, I needed help. As I said previously, I know my limitations, and I know when to ask for help. Analyzing contracts is not one of my strong suits beyond basic comprehension.

I had participated in a few small business growth programs offered through a few different universities. (More on this later.)

Therefore, I reached out to a contact from one of the schools. I was referred to a law school that partnered small businesses with law students. The students provided simple legal services to the business while gaining real-life experience—all under the watchful direction and guidance of seasoned law professors. They did not offer legal advice, but they could help with simple contract review and negotiations.

The school agreed to take me on for the semester and they reviewed the contract on my behalf. Afterward, they made several suggestions to my benefit. I sent the amended contract back to SAVOR and did not hear from them for more than a month. I followed up with a couple of emails and got crickets. I thought surely they were not agreeable to the changes, and the deal was off.

I was about to give up on the idea when I finally heard from the vice president with an apology for the delayed response and acknowledgement that the changes to the contract made good business sense. I was invited back to sign the contract and to work out the particulars, including how they would purchase the dry rubs to accurately execute the recipes. I breathed a huge sigh of relief. Although they did low-key ask for the recipes to my rubs—an idea I immediately dismissed.

My staff and I began perfecting recipes for the McCormick Place staff, and within several weeks the recipes were finalized and the production sheets and order guides were completed. Weeks later my chef manager and I returned to McCormick Place and worked on the recipes with their culinary team. We were all set to open in February 2019, three months prior to our second anniversary and a little over a year prior to a global pandemic.

The opening at McCormick Place was amazing and happened during a huge dental conference. I closed the restaurant so the entire staff could bask in the moment as a team and enjoy lunch at the food court. Although everyone was excited, this opportunity ended up not being exactly what I had anticipated. The amount of money we earned was miniscule and did not contribute to our bottom line. Being in the space was great for marketing, but honestly not for much else.

*****

When it comes to marketing, social media is a great tool offering several budget-friendly options for business owners to post information and "boost" those posts to reach a higher number of potential customers. Marketing is more than hiring a high-powered team of experts to help promote your business or services, it is essential to drawing the right kind of attention to your new business.

Most small businesses, particularly when first starting, simply do not have extra dollars earmarked for marketing and promoting. So, keep in mind there are many ways to do this and get your name out there while testing concepts and recipes.

Initially, I took advantage of several opportunities to work neighborhood festivals, as well as city, state, and other sponsored events—too many to name. In the summer it seems every one of Chicago's seventy-seven neighborhoods hosts a festival of some sort. Even when the event is not specific to food, there will *still* be food vendors present—from Rib Fest to Taste of Chicago, to Blues Fest, Gospel Fest, and Jazz Fest. If there are people gathered, a variety of good grub will not be far away. It is Chicago, after all. There is never a shortage of good food here.

The first major outdoor event my staff and I participated in was the annual four-day African Festival of the Arts sponsored by Africa International House USA, Inc., which is held in Washington Park over Labor Day weekend. We participated a couple of years after opening Evelyn's Food Love. This festival would bring in vendors of all types from across the country—clothes, arts, jewelry, you name it. Everything is represented and there is music and other artists to enjoy, as well as food vendors from across the city and well beyond. Thousands gather over the course of the four days to enjoy the vibrant scene, electric atmosphere and diverse dining options.

We signed on to participate about a week before the event. On the first day, my crew and I arrived early to set up our 10x10-feet space and everything was going fine. That is, until I observed other food vendors starting to arrive. I was taken aback. These vendors were rolling up in huge trucks and unloading serious kitchen equipment. I'm talking about commercial fryers, ovens, refrigerators, and freezers; they were setting up whole kitchens!

I glanced around at our chafing dishes and sterno and felt like exactly what I was: a complete amateur. I silently went into a full-blown panic. Although it was important to look competent on the outside – even if I was missing the mark within. I knew if I panicked, my staff might panic, too.

With a poker face, I internally devised a quick plan and started to execute. Other vendors were passing by, looking curiously at our space. I was surprised they weren't pointing and laughing at our meager set up.

The seasoned vendor who was set up next to us was friendly and helpful. She offered good advice and suggested the first day would be slow. But we were a new vendor and word spread quickly so we were non-stop busy from start to finish all four days. I was happy that the restaurant was a straight shot away, less than a ten-minute drive from the park. I had called the kitchen and instructed the staff to keep cooking until I told them to stop. The pot washer had become our runner, transporting fresh food to us as needed throughout the entire weekend.

We worked my impromptu plan the entire event. Staff cooked and routinely dropped off food from the restaurant, meaning our food was fresh and delicious at all times. Simultaneously, the staff assigned to the park served food and delighted customers for four completely packed festival days. Everyone, including casual observers, assumed this was the plan all along. Ha! Not even close.

My journal entry following the event was titled "Culinary Chronicles - Festivals" and read:

"After completing our very first multi-day event, I can honestly say I feel like I've been in a prize fight; and lost – BEFORE being run over by a Mack Truck, then tossed over the side of a jagged-edged cliff, hit by a freight train and knocked into

a muddy pond.... But I'd do it all over again so what does that say about, me, lol!"

I understood better after that event that asking the right questions—and of the right people—was paramount. I spent a good deal of time walking around, seeing what other food vendors were selling. I made mental notes about how their spaces were set up to prepare myself and my staff for any future events.

Fortunately, I had not bitten off more than I could chew for the festival weekend and no one panicked—at least not visibly. However, had the location been farther away from the restaurant, the results could have been disastrous and costly, especially to my reputation as a restaurateur and chef.

Nevertheless, we participated successfully in several more festivals afterward and they became a big part of our marketing plan. Efficiently getting in front of as many people and companies as possible turned out to be an effective marketing tool helping us to get our name out and for providing ongoing referrals and creating customer lists.

For instance, as the official tourism/marketing agency for the city, Choose Chicago brings national and international events, such as Lollapalooza and NASCAR, to Chicago and encourages participation for businesses of all sizes. Exposing your business to any of these ventures offers a great deal of publicity. However, it is imperative that you do your homework. Be sure to research and understand requirements, and start small before diving into the deep end. Avoid getting in over your head and having your business and reputation suffer because of lack of experience handling the volume or the pressure.

Also note: Do not hoard your business cards. You already know who you are and what you do. So anyone within a few feet of you is a potential customer. Tell and sell your business at every opportunity. Practice and tighten your one-minute elevator pitch that can quickly sum up who you are and what your business is about. A digital card can be stored in your phone and sent to someone in an instant with or without a barcode reader. Anyone can take a quick photo of your business card and save it immediately in their contacts, so give them out freely.

Okay… Maybe one more thing. A friend shared something from her experience working in the Black Press as an advertising account representative, speaking and working with small business owners on their marketing plans. She said in working with Black-owned businesses in the community, especially new businesses, owners often said the same thing when it came to marketing and advertising, "I rely on word of mouth." This was particularly common before social media became as popular as it is now. In her experience, she indicated she always told them the truth: "You cannot control word of mouth." Making an investment in telling your business' story is an investment in how you want your business to be perceived, and it extends the invitation from you to do business with you. More plainly, it invites customers to spend money in your restaurant and to enjoy great food. If you tell them repeatedly that your food is great, someone will believe it. Of course, it's better if it's true, but someone will believe you and accept your invitation to come and dine regardless.

Those owners who believe strictly in "word of mouth advertising" do not understand that what they were relying on is a narrative they are unable to control. "Word of mouth" can also destroy a business if someone has a large enough audience and perceived that they had a terrible experience with your establishment.

How you market your business and services is a part of doing business. It also helps with your exposure to the masses. An honest, compelling story about you and your business is paramount and perhaps not something that artificial intelligence can do thoroughly or accurately on your behalf.

Tell your story fully and maybe AI can help with enhancing it.

"Many of life's failures are people who did not realize how close they were to success when they gave up."

Thomas Edison

Chapter 8

Poppin' Up At Pop-Ups

By now, business was steady at Evelyn's Food Love. We served customers from all walks of life and from all over Chicago. Although the greater numbers had diminished, our regular customer base was forming.

Guests were constantly asking what we used to season our food. And with the seasonings we were selling to McCormick Place this would fuel another business idea later, which was selling our seasonings on a large scale through Consumer Packaged Goods or CPG which I will discuss later.

However, when one of our regular customers suggested we work with a food company that specialized in providing catered meals to office staff throughout the city, but mostly in the downtown area, I decided to look into pop-ups as another potential revenue stream. The opportunities were limitless.

I reached out to the company involved and was invited to their corporate office for a meeting and tasting. The team put together a few sample menu ideas with food costs tight enough for us to be profitable while paying the related fees. The company's management team and their staff were impressed with our menu options, with the projected menu prices falling within their price points—the amount their customers were comfortable spending on a lunch meal. One of their employees, who was from New Orleans, even said our etouffee was as good as any she ever had growing up and that it reminded her of home. With the success of that initial meeting, we began collaborating within weeks.

The first time we participated in a pop-up event we sold out early. Within a couple of months, Evelyn's Food Love was one of their top sellers, winning a few prizes—including personalized marketing materials, like professional banners and such. Companies were requesting our food specifically at their sites.

We later met a couple of minority business owners who showed us the ropes and demonstrated how we could negotiate better to acquire greater assignments. They advised us on what to look out for and which locations were the most profitable or needed to be steered clear of for various reasons. Several accounts paid for meals upfront, and they were the most desirable sites, as were the accounts that offered their employees free or discounted lunches. We were told restaurant owners and caterers could also choose which accounts they preferred and refuse other accounts altogether.

We began to better understand the pop-up process and how to make pop-ups a viable extension of our catering operation. We ended up working just a few profitable accounts a few days each week to maximize our earnings. Since most restaurants tend to perform slowly early in the week, we were closed on Mondays and Tuesdays and used the time to shop and prep for our customers the rest of the week. We then incorporated hosting pop-ups during lunch into the Monday – Wednesday schedule. I decided to hire a separate team to work the pop-ups exclusively early in the week to increase profitability.

We learned well how to best navigate the pop-up scene to the point where we were asked by the company to open several new accounts for them to impress their new clients. They also began using us in their higher volume, higher profile accounts, and in their corporate catering operations, which were quite profitable. This helped our bottom line tremendously, especially when the restaurant began to slow down from the publicity and when operations became more manageable. The company we worked with seemed well-versed in gaining corporate accounts, and they had little competition at the start.

However, the one-day events began taking a toll. Staff never knew what kind of space they would be asked to operate in, and sometimes those spaces could be untenable—a cold lobby, a cramped hallway, and once they even worked in a space that resembled an oversized closet. They made it work, but it became challenging. Often the schedule came out early in the month and included an estimated number of meals for the event. The estimate would diminish substantially, however, as the month progressed and the attractive numbers were simply no longer there.

On the day of the event, the number of meals originally projected would often have decreased by 40-60 percent, sometimes more. It started to feel like bait and switch. Bait us with the high numbers early on, then switch to the actual lower numbers later. This wreaked havoc on our food and labor costs as well as revenue. To offset this we began requesting specific assignments in specific locations and only on specific days of the week. Everything else was refused; it was simply not as profitable. With these types of pop-up events, a business owner has to truly drill down on the numbers to ensure success. A business also has to be okay with walking away if the numbers don't jibe. Like they say, if it doesn't make money, it doesn't make sense.

I then learned of another company that was doing something similar yet different. I reached out to them and learned that they were, in fact, part of a large food service management company—one of the largest in the world, one that I was very familiar with. And they were getting into the pop-up game.

After meeting with them, I became aware of their strategy to place restaurants and food partners in the same location for a full week instead of hosting a different event each day. Additionally, they paid their partners within 24 hours of an event. What was most appealing about this arrangement was that they made sure their restaurant partners had access to kitchens, food courts, pantries, storage and other amenities conducive to producing and providing meals in a cafeteria or restaurant-like setting—all in a safe and sanitized manner. *Hallelujah, no more closets!*

This partnership had great potential. I met vendors who were thrilled to work with this agency. One, in particular, said his Indian concept restaurant was failing until he partnered with this company. He made it his business to work, almost exclusively, with the company at multiple sites daily throughout the week. He said after about a year, his restaurant began to prosper because of the exposure he enjoyed the previous year from providing food at so many pop-ups. People knew him, and they knew where to find him. They enjoyed his food, and they supported his brick and mortar restaurant back into profitability. He had used pop-ups as a successful marketing tool.

It was all very encouraging and clearly doable. We partnered successfully in this space but only briefly, however. Evelyn's Food Love enjoyed a couple of successful events and experiences with this new collaboration. Except one experience with this company left us with a bad taste: A large, multi-day event was canceled the day before without a replacement assignment. Not only were we not informed, but we were also expected to eat the cost.

Food and supplies had been purchased to feed nearly 100 people per day for four days. There was no way I was losing that amount of money. I insisted they compensate me for lost revenue and for two days' wages for my staff. I advocated for myself and my team. Reluctantly, they agreed. Had I said nothing, neither would they have. That did not sit well with me.

I am quite particular about how I do business and with whom. For this reason, it was known that I would not stand for anything less than what my team and I deserved, which is why I am even more particular now. I continued to work with the initial company and was successfully juggling both by early 2020. I costed out the food and labor, drilled down on the numbers and they had proved profitable. I also thought about deploying multiple teams to multiple sites daily throughout the week.

Unexpectedly, by late March, things were changing. A global pandemic was looming and about to disrupt the world as we knew it. This disruption impacted the food industry in an unprecedented manner unfamiliar to everyone inside and outside of the industry.

"If you are feeling like you are beat up, knocked down, lost, burnt out, all alone, depressed or having any other negative feelings or thoughts ... I pray that you never give up your faith. For it will always protect you through the darkest of days."

-Daymond John, Businessman/Investor

Chapter 9

Global Pandemic, Big Opportunity

Things had slowed considerably as the uncertainty of the pandemic continued to loom. People were not always taking social distancing seriously, and I recall a St. Patrick's Day party at a local restaurant causing the mayor and the governor to call for the immediate closing of restaurants. Wait! What?! *If my restaurant closes, I can't make money. If I can't make money, I can't pay the mortgage. If I can't pay the mortgage, not only do I lose the restaurant, I also lose my house. The same house that, against my better judgment, I used as collateral to fund my dream.*

This was a mess, but what could I do? I certainly could not control a global pandemic, and I am not one to spend a single second worrying about something I have no control over. So, right then, I decided that would be my excuse (or reason) when I lost everything. I was going to file for bankruptcy, get a regular job and return to corporate, and then disappear into an abyss of shame while blaming the pandemic that was beyond my control for my epic failure.

That was it.

That was the plan.

I just had to put together a quick exit strategy, decide on a closing date, give my staff notice, and execute. Simple. At least that is what I thought at the time.

I was at a pop-up with my staff, trying to get a feel for what was going on. We were working at what would be, unbeknownst to us, one of our final pop-up events. It was in a location that had always been quite profitable. The event was so slow that we left with nearly all of the food we arrived with. We began chilling down all of the food on-site, as we realized business just wasn't there; employees who had patronized us previously were scarce. COVID-19 was running rampant, but we were still hopeful because some of the chilled down food could be used the following day for another scheduled event at a hospital. The rest of the food we would donate as we so often did.

Though social distancing and universal precautions were now globally expected, they were always the norm in healthcare. When we arrived on location the next day, our temperatures were taken upon entrance, and we had to maintain a distance of six feet apart. Masks and gloves were mandatory in the facility, but this was something my staff was accustomed to prior to the pandemic.

Once we reached our destination and set up, we waited. And waited. *Nothing*. By this time, lunch was in full effect, and the cafeteria was eerily quiet—more so dead. A few customers trickled in during the first hour, but shortly after we learned that some company had donated food to the entire hospital and everyone was in the lobby, partaking in the generous gesture.

At this point, most restaurants throughout the city had already closed or switched to pre-prepared meals for pick-up only or curbside delivery. Things were changing, and we needed to start changing also. So, I decided that when we returned to the restaurant, I would inform my staff that I could likely only keep them on payroll for another two weeks, three tops. I was planning to shut down operations; COVID had won.

While at the hospital event my phone started buzzing. I would typically not answer while working, but the caller was persistent, having called multiple times before I finally checked. I decided to answer when my phone vibrated again, after all, it was almost a ghost town.

I answered the call and the voice on the other end was the executive director with my lender. Yes, LISC was still looking out for my small business. The caller sounded excited, explaining that she had been trying to reach me. She almost shouted, "Is your restaurant still open?! I have an opportunity for you!" I told her I was still open, and she shared that a Major League Baseball team in the city wanted to make sure that people had food. They were looking for restaurants and catering partners for their charitable arm, Chicago Cubs Charities, on the South Side.

She suggested our restaurant could be helpful, and someone from the charity wanted to have a discussion to understand our capacity and how we could potentially partner. I looked at my staff and breathed a deep sigh of relief. They had no idea how close they had come to a decidedly different outcome. They had families and responsibilities and depended on our success to make a living. Depending on what the sports team needed, I would not have to lay anyone off… At least not within the next two weeks.

It felt good to exhale.

Chapter 10

When The Dotted Line Becomes A Lifeline

When the charity called later that day, I learned that we would be preparing about 100 to 200 meals per day, five days per week for about a month. Cubs Charities would provide containers for the meals to be individually packaged, delivery boxes to pack the food, and a driver to pick everything up daily at noon. This meant we could work within their modest budget and still be profitable if I priced our menus appropriately, which I did.

With swift calculation, I deduced I could pay my staff for a couple of months giving them ample time to look for other employment if they chose—given the uncertainty of the pandemic. I could also pay off my business associate in full and return the emergency check my friend had previously written to me that was still uncashed. Furthermore, I was able to start paying off most of the credit card debt I had personally incurred early on.

We did well enough with the meals requested that the contract was extended a few weeks longer than the original agreement. The agency for whom we were providing the meals also extended the contract out of their own budget for yet another couple of weeks. They then received funding from one of their other supporters for an additional week or so. Because of that project, my finances were good for several months, and I gave my staff the option of continuing to work until there was no more work or moving on if they wanted or needed to. Some opted to stay, and a couple opted to leave. Understandably, they were leaving Chicago to ride out the pandemic with their families in other parts of the country.

A few months into COVID-19, and after our initial contracts, we received another necessary lifeline that we used for salaries and other expenses—a bridge grant from The University of Chicago (U of C), our first. At that point, we were on track to generate more revenue that year than we had the previous two years of normal operations. Even in the face of an unexpected global crisis, the blessings just kept coming. (Look at God!)

The U of C grant came shortly prior to an opportunity to work with Chef José Andrés' food relief agency, World Central Kitchen (WCK), through a company called Off Their Plate. Evelyn's Food Love was referred by U of C with whom we had a relationship and previously catered multiple events at their Hyde Park campus, including an event hosted by Chase Bank featuring the CEO of JP Morgan Chase, Jaime Dimon.

U of C referred Off Their Plate to us to help them in their efforts to supply meals to first responders. We partnered with them to prepare meals for recipients in various locations throughout the South Side. We were preparing and dropping off, by now, a few hundred meals daily to various healthcare agencies.

Disaster relief companies, such as Off Their Plate, successfully leveraged existing infrastructures inside restaurant and catering kitchens. Their goal was to dispatch meals quickly and efficiently in emergency situations while supporting local businesses. With help from my bookkeeper and accountant, I had been running my business strategically from the start. In addition to filing and paying taxes, I developed good collaborative business and community relationships by providing excellent food and professional service consistently. Laying the groundwork properly was paying off. Our name was being spoken in rooms when we were not present and in the best possible way.

It was also during this time that we "adopted" a community hospital near the restaurant. Evelyn's Food Love had physically closed, but we had food in our freezers. We began preparing and then donating meals to the emergency room staff at the hospital. They were seeing unprecedented numbers of patients during the pandemic and rarely had time to break for meals outside of the facility.

We sent lunch one afternoon, and before we arrived back at the restaurant the staff had left a voice message expressing their gratitude. One nurse was saying thank you, and we could hear the tears in her voice. We decided then to provide them with meals each week until we ran out of food.

After about five or six weeks, we asked Cubs Charities to provide lunch for the entire hospital. They eagerly agreed to do so, provided we prepared the meals—win-win. This was one of the 'feel-good' things we did for the community to show our gratitude for their support. We continue this now by hiring within the community and hosting events that teach some, or train others. We also hold community-wide anniversary celebrations and food giveaways, during which we have treated the neighborhood children to treats, drinks and snacks. In addition, free desserts and live entertainment also serve as a continuation of our efforts to help bring the neighborhood together to share in the upward mobility for us all.

During the pandemic and because of operating the business legitimately, we were afforded opportunities that businesses operating under the radar could not access. I was extremely grateful. When grants and other financial opportunities, like contracts, began surfacing during COVID-19, I was prepared and typically applied successfully. I qualified for and received, multiple grants in addition to a low interest Paycheck Protection Program (PPP) loan. I refrained from accessing the maximum amount we qualified for simply because of the uncertainty of COVID and not knowing what might be waiting on the other side of the pandemic. I played it safe and waited for more grants to surface and eventually they did.

Due to the pandemic and our SBA loan, I also qualified for certain automatic federal relief funds and other assistance. This included the Economic Injury Disaster Loans (EIDL). The federal government took over the mortgage payments on the restaurant for eight months in 2020, and then an additional five or six months in 2021. I thought they would tack the payments onto the back of the loan, but no, they were *actually* paying down the mortgage! I could not believe my blessing, considering I had previously been contemplating bankruptcy as part of my exit plan.

When I began to repay the loan, at some point in early 2022, my accountant and I realized the balance was within reach of being paid off completely. I had been stacking cash for months without a mortgage payment and was well positioned to pay off the balance in full and quickly disentangle my home from my business.

This would be the biggest relief to come in the nearly two years since the pandemic. Having a fully paid for, unencumbered, commercial property allowed me to go about my business in the least stressful manner possible. Only having to deal with taxes and insurance ensured peace of mind that I had not experienced since opening—a peace of mind that most restaurant owners could only imagine. While one of my accountants disagreed with me paying off the mortgage, viewing it as wiser to accrue interest on the extra funds, I chose to move forward with paying off the balance post-haste.

PART THREE

The Breakthrough

Chapter 11

Mo' Business, Mo' Money

While still preparing meals for first responders and others in need, another opportunity presented itself in the spring of 2022. A good friend and colleague, working as a general manager for a large food service management company, did not renew her contract with a small social service agency managing their food service operation. She approached me and asked if I was interested in acquiring the contract. At the absolute least, I wanted to learn more. After all, she was giving it up because it was not a profitable venture so why would I be interested?

I reached out to the Chief Financial Officer (CFO) of the corporation via email, and my friend connected me to the Executive Vice President (EVP) on site at the facility. I was later invited to bid on the contract, and I did. Then, I waited.

A short while later, the agency reached out to me to see if I could cater meals until they worked through the bid process. I agreed to assist for a couple of weeks, working with the cook who was still their employee. When the previous operators left, they also took their business license to operate the kitchen with them. This meant meals could no longer be prepared on site in the kitchen at the facility.

Evelyn's Food Love began cooking meals for our clients in our kitchen and dropping off pans of prepared food for their cook to plate and serve in their kitchen. After two weeks of service, I was asked to extend our assistance for a couple of months. By then, their cook had begun working in our kitchen while I put together a rotating, five-week cycle menu of three meals and two snacks per day—all of which were to be individually packaged, transported in insulated containers, held hot in food warmers, and served whenever the clients were ready to eat. I worked out a reasonable catering fee that the contractors found agreeable. It was both reasonable and profitable in the long run.

I was able to streamline the old process to the point where our food and labor costs were nominal since the menus were simple enough to execute. One person could complete the entire days' menus in a few hours with time to prep for the rest of the week. This was a seven-day operation, including weekends and holidays.

For holiday meals, the EVP wanted her clients to have a more upscale and traditional dining experience, and we charged our normal catering prices for those events. They would also engage us for various other catering opportunities, like meetings and staff appreciation events. This proved to be a profitable arrangement with minimal labor and food costs. Reduced food costs meant cooks could earn a livable wage.

Along with our other catering events and contracts, I saw positive cash flow that allowed Evelyn's Food Love to pay off our remaining debt, including start-up costs and credit cards I had maxed out. With investors and the mortgage balance paid, I now owned my business and the building outright. This would prove useful when later applying for grants, business loans, and lines of credit, providing me immense peace of mind.

Again, my team and I worked with the facility for the initial two weeks they had requested before they asked if we could extend our services for a couple more months. A short time later, they received substantial funding to make capital improvements to the facility, including a new kitchen, servery, and cafeteria. Those couple of months extended to more than two years of providing meals for their clients before the facility was ultimately shut down by the State of Illinois for reasons unrelated to food or nutrition.

During that time, I strategically negotiated a better price per meal, per person. It was less than the amount I normally charge for catering, less than what I was paid when working with the state during the migrant crisis, and less than what I was paid when feeding first responders during the start of the pandemic. It was, however, more volume for a longer period. This translated into more profit in the long run. Paying a cook to produce consistently good meals in a timely manner, hiring a pot washer who could keep the place clean and prep, and paying both better than just livable wages was a great incentive for them both and worked to my advantage. Remaining efficient, streamlining menus and processes, and preventing unnecessary waste kept us profitable the entire time.

Additionally, one day each week we offered a cold menu for breakfast and lunch—Danishes, boiled eggs, cold cereal, milk, juice, yogurt and such for breakfast bags. For lunch, hoagies or other cold sandwiches—along with chips, salad, coleslaw, and such—were served. We incorporated fast food into the rotation to deliver a hot dinner—generally pizza and wings, or pasta, or fried foods (like fish) that were not offered on any of our regular menus.

This modification meant that everyone was off on Mondays and could rotate weekends. Occasionally, I included some Fridays during the summer. It was the perfect arrangement; clients were pleased, and this afforded me the flexibility needed to conduct business across the board.

Again, this contract, which was initially meant to last only two months, ended up lasting over two years. I like to think it was because we made working with us very easy. Remaining flexible and adjusting as needed or requested worked well. I offered a fair price for our services, showed up every day on or before time, and never missed a single day servicing this client during the entire contract.

All of the cooks and chefs were quite consistent with our recipes, just as we had learned while operating the restaurant. Not using recipes at home is your choice, while not using recipes in your restaurant could quite possibly equate to business suicide. Consistency is key and nothing is more annoying than going to your favorite restaurant for your favorite meal only to learn that a different cook prepared it a different way and missed the mark entirely.

Contracts kept me in business and kept Evelyn's Food Love on the map, during the entire pandemic. I was forced to see and operate my business differently and being nimble worked to my advantage.

I recall seeing one restaurant owner on the local news after he had been awarded a contract. He was emotional and honest when he relayed to the reporter that for the first time since opening his business, he was able to fully operate his business the way a business should operate in order to be successful. I could relate. Still, there is one contract that I have tried and failed to acquire. In fact, it continues to elude me to this day.

*****

Years ago, I visited two young women in an Ohio prison. I had often acted as a youth motivational speaker in some of the public schools as a corporate employee. So, of course, I was happy to visit and support two young women who had made mistakes, like many of us do.

When I asked them both if there was anything I could do for them while I was there, I fully expected one, or both, to ask for things like keeping in touch, magazines, phone cards, or something similar. I was thoroughly surprised when, almost in unison, they asked for chicken wings. *Wait. What? Chicken wings?*

Apparently, chicken wings were a treat and could be purchased from the adjacent room that was filled with a bank of vending machines that sold various food items. To my surprise, there were no chicken wings in the vending machines. Zero, zip, nada on the wings for the three days I visited. This got me thinking.

Who has the contract to supply wings to prisons?

Certainly, if I had the contract, there would never be a wing shortage, and I knew this.

I began imagining how to pull it off: A grant to purchase a warehouse, banks of fryers, coolers and blast chillers, ample storage, large prep area, and refrigerated vans for delivery. This could work. But where would I start? That would prove to be the million-dollar question since this topic was not easily Googleable, nor did most people I'd ask have any concrete information about prison vending machine contracts.

I pondered this question for years (yes, years) until the day I ended up seated next to a lobbyist while attending a conference. We somehow got onto the subject of prison vending contracts, and I explained my interest and challenges in getting good information about said machines. The lobbyist shared that those particular contracts are 100% held by "blind vendors." *Blind vendors?*

I asked, confused, "Why would the contracts be secret?"

He asked, equally confused, "Secret?"

"Yes, you said blind; did you mean secret?" I asked, still confused. It was starting to feel like an Abbott and Costello 'Who's on First?' skit.

He chuckled before clarifying that he meant blind, as in "visually impaired."

Now, I was really confused. How are visually impaired individuals preparing meals? And, perhaps more importantly, how did they get 100% of the contracts? Not 50% or 75%... 100%.

I left the event, just as perplexed as ever, with no real answer or solution to my query. I got a bit closer when I began working with a group of U of C students who work with small business owners to solve a problem as part of their coursework. I asked them to investigate prison vending food contracts, and they did. Their finished report, titled "Breaking into Prisons," provided me with some insight into the blind vendors, stakeholders, and potential negotiation tactics to pursue this matter further, which I will eventually do.

So, while I am no closer to breaking through (or breaking into) prison vending contracts, I am leaving this option open for further exploration.

Chapter 12

Business Enterprise Program (BEP) Certification

I began working on my Business Enterprise Program (BEP) certifications early on. Evelyn's Food Love is Airport Concession Disadvantaged Business Enterprise (ACDBE), Disadvantaged Business Enterprise (DBE), Minority Business Enterprise (MBE), and Women's Business Enterprise (WBE) certified. You could say I am all the BE's I can be. I was told to do this because it was necessary to acquire certain contracts with the city, state, county, and federal government, as well as various private agencies. I understood contracts to be a viable way to generate alternate streams of revenue that could be very lucrative. As that is the whole point of being in business, considerable effort and resources were made to make this happen.

I connected with an amazing professional, who worked at the Chicago Urban League. This was her specific area of expertise, and she was making some "folk" wealthy with her vast knowledge of BEP certification and the procurement process. She basically held my hand and walked me through the process while sharing information about other businesses she had coached to million-dollar status. I was pretty sure I would never let her out of my sight, and I have not to this day although, she has since moved on to bigger opportunities.

This person connected me to a Black-owned agency that, at the time, was helping small and minority-owned businesses to become certified at no cost. I found the paperwork and process daunting and time consuming because, at the time, I was still working *in* my business while trying to work *on* my business. I had no idea when I would have the time to focus exclusively on the task of becoming certified without assistance.

I was given the name of a gentleman to contact, and we made an immediate appointment to get started. He informed me of what I should bring to the meeting and said, "Any legitimate business should have this information." Choosing to overlook his phrasing, I collected the requested information and documents. When we met a week later, I was ready. I had paper documents as well as my laptop, just in case I forgot something or had to get onto some agency's website to retrieve information.

Equipped with his laptop, we sat in the conference room of his office and started the application process. He asked me a series of questions, which I answered with ease. At the end of an hour, much to my surprise, he had nearly completed the application for our business certification.

He then provided me with a short list of items I needed to provide at our next meeting to fully complete the application. I returned, much to his surprise, less than a week later with the additional information. He seemed impressed that I was taking everything so seriously, and he said as much.

With the application completed, he printed the documents. He then downloaded everything onto a portable drive for me to take with me, which later came in handy. He would soon mail everything to the first certifying agency, and I would wait to hear from them to schedule an in-person interview at the restaurant. That was part of the process, presumably, to prevent any fraud in awarding businesses with government contracts.

When I applied for certification with other agencies, that portable drive contained everything I needed to streamline the processes. Typically, most agencies ask for the same information, with a few exceptions. Some may require a few more pieces of information, others a few less, but the bulk of the information is relatively the same. So, completing the process once is usually all that is necessary to obtain multiple certifications.

Once I sat for the initial certification interview, I went about the business of getting certified through the city, state, and federal government, respectively. They are all largely free or charge a nominal amount. Many offer reciprocity that allow certification between agencies if either have already certified your business.

I also sought certification through private agencies that charge annual fees and host annual conferences, and meet-and-greet opportunities with the companies with whom they do business. Those companies, in turn, offer opportunities to conduct business with small, certified companies like mine.

I kept our certifications up to date and active even though I did not see the benefit initially. I had previously bid on a few contracts and attended multiple culinary cohorts that focused on helping small businesses secure government contracts, all to no avail. The process appeared rather complicated and convoluted, to be frank. It also seemed to exclude the very people who were supposed to be included and benefit from the bidding process—

hence the many rules and regulations associated with getting certified.

I later learned that in previous years, non-minorities were awarded contracts through deceit. As it turned out, some men had claimed their wives were the heads of their corporations or 51% owners to acquire the MBE or WBE status and related contracts when that was simply not the case. And although it struck me as funny when I began the certification process, it made sense why I had to literally prove that I am precisely what anyone with eyes can clearly see: Black and female.

Chapter 13

Nourishing Folks Using State Contracts

Being certified did come in handy for the McCormick Place opportunity and again in late summer of 2022. This is when large numbers of migrants began pouring into "sanctuary cities" en masse. So, imagine my surprise when staff from state government agencies, who previously claimed they had no idea how to find our business, suddenly not only knew how to find us but were reaching out directly via cell phone. They wanted to encourage me to apply for short-term contracts to feed migrants or staff in facilities that were housing migrants. In other words, they will find you if *they* need you.

Since we were already catering quite a bit, I opted to feed staff at a few migrant shelters that were located in close proximity to the restaurant, but not before learning what the payment schedule would be. I'd heard horror stories about businesses folding while waiting on payments from government agencies. And I'd escaped enough close calls.

Fortunately, I had enough cash on hand to fulfill a government contract from the previous contract work we had acquired. Still, I needed to get paid in a timely manner if I was expected to foot upfront costs to provide these meals. Therefore, my team and I negotiated and thoroughly explained the plight of small businesses. The state agreed to receive invoices weekly and to make payments every two weeks and, to their credit, they did. *You have not, because you ask not.*

I found the contracts to be exceptionally profitable and calculated that even a year-long agreement would have been worth more than seven figures. The state, however, made it abundantly clear that these were short-term deals so I could beat it with my champagne wishes and caviar dreams. I later learned also that the contract administration would be transferred to and carried out by the city and for considerably less money. The restaurant was not big enough—nor was our kitchen big enough—to handle super low-paying, super high volume, mass meal production. I would have been happy to partner with a bigger agency, but that opportunity did not present.

These state contracts, or any contract for that matter, could positively change businesses, communities and lives. They provide opportunities that already exist, just unfortunately not for everyone. However, contracts forced us to work efficiently, and we still routinely bid. With the short-term bids we did acquire, the staff was able to convert the dining room at the restaurant into an assembly line. We would first drop off lunch for the day. Later, we would drop off dinner and a continental breakfast for the following morning. We were getting calls from companies as far away as O'Hare International Airport, which is a considerable distance from our location, asking if we could take them on as clients also.

We were unable to accept the business at O'Hare because getting to the airport can be difficult even when traffic conditions are favorable. Lunchtime traffic could make traveling to the airport every day, in a timely manner, a challenge we simply could not meet without the proper resources including reliable transportation. In business it is equally important to know precisely when to say "no," to preserve the good name of your business. "Not all money is good money," as the saying goes. So, we did decline a few opportunities. Instead, opting to keep our reputation (and newly found sanity) intact. In the end, I made the most of several short-term, well-paying state contracts as well as the two-year contract we acquired, and I never had to lay off any staff. In fact, I added agency and other temporary staff members whenever extra hands were needed. Any debt related to opening the business was completely paid off within five years of opening, and there was positive cash flow. This would come in handy when I began applying for grants to expand the space and began developing my dry rubs to sell business-to-business.

*****

Speaking of contracts. We were able to become an approved vendor with the Chicago Public Schools (CPS) purely by happenstance. I explained this to a small business owner after I purchased a meal that I was dissatisfied with from his restaurant. I originally intended to chalk up the experience and let it go as I often do, but I decided instead to inform him of my discontent just in case he was unaware of any issues. Or, hopefully, if he was interested in potential solutions. As a business owner, I appreciate honest feedback.

Some restaurants, while trying to be mindful of food costs will often repurpose leftovers. In many instances this is perfectly fine. However there are other instances when certain food items are simply not as good the next day or any other day unless they have been creatively reimagined. For example, pork shoulder is perfectly delicious as a pulled pork sandwich the next day. So is chicken prepared as chilled chicken salad, in a tasty stir fry, in a hearty soup or in many other delicious applications.

At Evelyn's Food Love, we regularly donate leftovers to various neighborhood agencies and prepare fresh meals daily, always striving to keep the main thing, the main thing. We are also mindful of batch cooking, which requires preparing most foods in small batches throughout the day and prevents overproducing which can lead to excessive waste.

We identified several facilities where we could drop off an occasional free lunch resulting from leftovers. This includes hospitals, political offices, police stations and, yes, schools. After making a few lunch donations to a local high school the principal inquired whether we were approved CPS vendors. Upon learning we were not, he then offered to sponsor our application, which was quickly approved as sponsorship from a principal was required.

This simple act of goodwill ended up benefitting our business financially in the long run. The restaurant owner, whose food I did not enjoy, understood the point and offered to replace my meal and make a few adjustments to his processes.

"The most valuable thing you can make is a mistake; you can't learn anything from being perfect.

Adam Osborne

Chapter 14

Mind Your Taxes & Your Accountant

Of all the lessons I have learned, during this entire process, and there have been many, hands down, top of the list is keeping track of and paying taxes—all of them. Property taxes, payroll taxes, income taxes, and sales taxes... Pay them. Even if you have an accountant, unless you have worked together for years and know your accountant well, always, always, always keep track of your taxes. Make sure they are filed and paid on time, every time.

I neglected to do this, and I learned the hard way what a colossal mistake I made. Not checking on or following up with my accountant regularly to make sure my business' taxes were being filed and paid cost me a bundle in penalties and fees. Reasonably, I thought the person I was paying was doing what they were being paid to do. I was busy taking care of the business and entrusted the accountant to take care of the taxes, rightfully. I did not learn this was not happening until the IRS showed up at the front door of the restaurant late one afternoon.

I was the last person in the restaurant that particular day, and I was locking the front gate when I saw a nondescript, rather ordinary looking man approaching. I was about to tell him we were closed for the day when he flashed his IRS badge and demanded entry. I was so taken aback that I opened the gate while still staring at his badge.

He brought to my attention that my sales taxes had not been filed or paid—in months. This was significant because that would have been shortly after our first television appearance. Business had been great for months, so the taxes would have been substantial. I was completely caught off guard by this unannounced visit and could not dispute what he was saying. I simply did not know, and I had no information to counter his claim. I suddenly could not even recall the last time I had spoken to my accountant. It had to have been fairly recent because the accountant was also responsible for payroll, and everyone was getting paid.

The IRS agent was unassuming but equally no-nonsense. He said, "Ma'am, you can't operate a business and not pay taxes. That's illegal, and we can shut you down. People have gone to jail for not paying taxes…" He spoke calmly yet directly, never raising his voice. He actually seemed annoyed that he had to leave wherever he left to come to my place of business and explain this. *Gone to jail? What on earth?*

Did I look like Al Capone to him?

Was he accusing me of tax evasion? *Was* I a tax evader?

Now, I could have just said I would look into this immediately and did just that. But *no*, instead I said, "Well if you shut me down, I really won't be able to pay the taxes now, will I?" He had clearly heard this before and without missing a breath or a beat, retorted, "We'll shut you down, *and* you'll pay."

He then dropped his card on the table like one would dop a mic while admonishing me to stay in contact. He added that if I did not stay in contact, he would return to tape off the front entrance. Apparently, if I removed the tape, I could be arrested, *geez*.

The agent walked out just as casually as he had walked in not 10 minutes prior. I followed him through the door, locked the gate, and considered never, ever reopening it again. I'd always heard stories about how "gangster" the IRS could be and there I was witnessing it firsthand.

I immediately spoke to a financial advisor, who recommended a new accountant who worked specifically with small business owners. After I met with the accountant, all my taxes were properly amended, refiled, and sent to the IRS with a request for a payment plan. I owed so much money that I had no idea how I would ever pay it back.

I couldn't even blame the first accountant. I could, but I should have been paying attention. I should have known sooner rather than later that there was a problem, and I didn't. That's on me, and I accepted responsibility so that I could move on quickly and not make that mistake again, and I never have. As my mother would say, "Bought sense is the best sense in the world." And that lesson cost me dearly.

Each day after that incident, I required the manager to run ad hoc tax reports and remove the sales taxes from the regular daily deposit—first. Those funds were deposited into a separate "tax" account every day and that account existed until we became financially stable enough to no longer require a separate account.

It took nearly two years, and some of the many financial benefits that came during the pandemic, to resolve my tax issues. A good accountant is integral to your small business, and I have the same one today who helped me to correct those initial problems. As my current accountant so aptly put it, "If you're making a little bit of money, you'll pay a little bit of taxes. If you are making a lot of money, then you should count yourself blessed and pay your taxes."

It goes without saying that if your business is profitable, you can't keep all the money; taxes must be paid. Avoid tax issues from the start. Price your menus to cover all of your expenses including, most importantly – taxes. Get a skilled bookkeeper to help with monthly profit and loss statements, balance sheets, and cash flow statements. Meet with your bookkeeper monthly and your accountant at least quarterly.

Once you find yourself in tax trouble, it can be quite challenging to extricate yourself—mostly because of the never-ending fees and penalties. This will ultimately amount to far more than the original tax debt. *It simply is not worth it.*

Chapter 15

The Business Of Acquiring Grants

A couple of years into the pandemic, grants were swirling around like dollar bills in a carnival cash booth. These grants were crucial to the survival and success of many small businesses that were still holding on by a thin thread—businesses that were not only looking to stay open but also to expand. The grants covered the costs of everything from new construction and storefront buildouts to various repairs and certain soft costs, like supplies, inventory, and salary.

I am always surprised by the number of small businesses that do not apply for grants. Grants, which do not have to be repaid, are always preferable to me over loans, which require repayment *and* interest. Some applications are simple and straight forward. Others are the opposite and may take several weeks or even months to complete. It is still worth the effort to apply for a chance at free money that your business may not otherwise have access to. While there are no guarantees that a particular business will win an award, you will absolutely not win an award if you do not apply.

I have applied for several grants during and since the pandemic that the city and various other agencies offered. I made no assumptions about who was more likely to be awarded a grant or in which communities. None of that, I just applied. I did not hire a grant writer; not even AI would be helpful in capturing important or subtle nuances in this case. I simply told my story as clearly and honestly as I could. I simply did not believe anyone else could tell my story better than me. I included my goals for using the funds, which encompassed ensuring staff and customer safety by expanding the space, continuing to make positive contributions to the community through free holiday meal giveaways, hiring from the community, and so much more.

While I did not engage a grant writer, I did get assistance with financial projections from my accountant and an amazing community organization whose mission included helping small businesses on the South Side, to revitalize those neighborhoods through economic growth and development. In fact, the Greater Chatham Initiative (GCI) assisted my small business on more than one occasion by constantly ensuring that I was aware of grant opportunities, hosting workshops to ensure small businesses had assistance, and helping to complete grant applications. Our restaurant is not located in their immediate service area, yet they still offered assistance. GCI is such a valuable resource in the community, and they offer their services at no cost to small businesses.

GCI reviewed my grant applications and made suggestions for improvements. They made referrals to architects, contractors, and others that I would need to move my project forward. Later, when an opportunity presented for us to grow our business through the sale of our seasonings and dry rubs, GCI was there to ensure I had properly priced our products for profitability and double-checked that our nutrition labels were accurate.

The Small Business Improvement Fund (SBIF) was the first and most approachable grant that I applied for. The requirements were simple enough: Complete a short application to apply for a grant up to $150,000 with a 10% cost share. I applied and was on the verge of getting approved when I discontinued the application for a chance at a different opportunity.

The Neighborhood Opportunity Fund (NOF) offered a larger award than the SBIF grant. The small NOF grant (really a forgivable loan) went up to $250,000 with a 25% cost share. Evelyn's Food Love was later awarded a NOF grant for just under $200,000 before I declined the award to apply for the NOF grant, which started at $250,000 and went up to $2.5 million, the following year.

After applying for the larger NOF grant, my initial application was denied. I was not dissuaded. I subsequently made several recommended tweaks to the application before reapplying when the grant reopened a few months later. On the second attempt, I was successful and won a substantial award during the summer of 2024 to expand the restaurant by adding a rooftop deck and bar with additional seating and a second bathroom. Stairs are necessary to access the space as well as an elevator to ensure Americans with Disabilities Act (ADA) compliance.

Every application inquired about property ownership or site control, specifically whether the applicant owned or leased the property for which they were applying for funds. This is likely the case for several reasons, including avoiding legal issues. If the grant is to make leasehold or capital improvements to the property, for example, does the applicant have the right or permission to do so if they do not legally own the property?

The larger problem could be potentially making substantial improvements to someone else's property and then losing the lease because of rent increases or an inability to maintain the business after the improvements are made. How tragic would it be to put a couple hundred thousand dollars into a property that you do not own, only to have the landlord triple the rent and boot you out after you've made a capital investment in his space using your grant or forgivable loan? Perhaps owning the property or having a long-term lease makes sense for a stronger grant application.

Please note also that when applying for grants or funds through the city, you cannot be indebted to the city. You cannot owe for a past due water bill, parking ticket—nothing. It does not matter how much or how little is owed.

I applied for the smaller grants initially because that is what our resources would support, at the time, given the cost share requirements. As time passed and my business finances became stronger, I applied for larger grants offering larger awards. This also came with a higher cost share, which could be problematic for small businesses—specifically those that are minority owned or located in underserved communities. This is a huge barrier for most small business owners.

These barriers are also why it is imperative that small businesses are honest about what can realistically be accomplished with the resources they have available. Many restaurants (the percentages vary) fail within the first few years of opening for several reasons, mostly financial.

Ask yourself the following questions. All of this and more should be considered in order to open and operate your restaurant successfully.

Do you have enough funds to get your business comfortably off the ground?

Are you skilled at costing out your menu to ensure you can generate enough profit to support all of your monthly expenses, including rent, utilities, food, labor, taxes etc.?

Do you have enough money in the bank for the lean times? (There are *always* lean times.)

Is your credit good enough to get a small business loan or business line of credit to help with operating or unexpected expenses? I acquired a business line of credit early on—when we did not need it, but qualified—and I will not use it until we begin the expansion project.

Are you proficient with accounting, or can you afford to pay a bookkeeper to help you keep track of your monthly expenses and finances?

Can you write a compelling story about yourself and your business? Can you write your story without the use of Artificial Intelligence which may not capture some of the nuances specific to you and your business?

If you answered "yes" then you may be ready.

Chapter 16

Consumer Packaged Goods (CPG)

One of the most frequent questions my staff and I were asked in the restaurant and during catered events was, "What is your food seasoned with?" I was generally encouraged to put the products on the market after responding with, "We make our seasonings in-house, in small batches, without excessive salt, additives or preservatives."

Going into retail was never the goal. Although I may be more inclined to do so if it happens organically sometime in the future.

I admit that retail is not of great interest to me because I participated in a couple of culinary cohorts that focused specifically on retail and there were enough unpleasant stories recounted to deter anyone from pursuing this option. My experience working with McCormick Place, though not particularly profitable in general, taught me the value of selling products in bulk. It similarly enlightened me that pursuing business-to-business opportunities is perhaps a better way to focus my efforts when scaling.

I seek out free resources first, then pay for related resources as needed. Through a good friend, I learned about an organization that attempts to connect small businesses to large corporations, specifically businesses operating in the healthy food space. We qualified because our seasonings are delicious and more importantly, salt-sensible which falls on the low end of the spectrum between no sodium and too much sodium. Through this agency we were able to connect to large organizations such as schools, colleges, universities, healthcare and various other facilities interested in healthier food options for their clients.

Having worked as an executive chef in healthcare facilities, I would frequently experiment with and mix ingredients for use in our retail and catering operations. The first seasoning I developed was created by blending several ingredients from partially empty containers and adding a few herbs and a bit of salt. It was a huge hit, but I could not remember every ingredient, any of the quantities or immediately duplicate the magic. I quickly learned a valuable lesson.

With the third or fourth attempt, everything was measured, written down, tweaked, worked, and reworked until a master product was developed from which subsequent products could also be crafted. My all-purpose seasoning and rubs are exclusively used in the restaurant with several other seasoning blends, including popular favorites like seafood, coffee rub and Cajun. All affectionately known as "Love Rubs." (I've heard all the jokes!)

At the time of this writing, I am discussing a potential contract with a major agency to carry our flavorful salt-sensible products for use in their kitchens.

"Chase the vision, not the money. The money will end up following you."

***-Tony Hsieh*ns*

Conclusion

If you've read this far and you're still thinking about opening a restaurant, there's still time to reconsider. Kidding!

However, keep in mind the restaurant business can be pretty fickle and an expensive venture to boot. Restaurants have an insatiable appetite for money—for munching on crisp dollar bills in mind boggling quantities, every denomination, every day, all day long.

Hear me clearly… Restaurants will chow down on your cash with reckless abandon. Rent, utilities, insurance, taxes, food, payroll, repairs… All have to be fed and fed regularly.

If opening a restaurant is where your heart is, then you should keep an open mind, stay flexible, and pivot when necessary. It is also a good idea to get comfortable with delegating.

Delegating is a business owner's best friend. Sure, your business may be your "baby," but babies occasionally need sitters. It's only hard to let go the first time. After that, you'll be handing that kid off every chance you get to the highly competent, well-paid manager who you trained personally.

Do you enjoy taking vacations? Delegate.

Do you like dining out? Delegate.

If you ever plan to take a day off, or plan to scale your business, you will have to entrust your baby to others. So, delegate!

You will often hear businesspeople say, "You have to work *on* your business and not *in* your business." That is often easier said than done, particularly for a new business owner just starting out. Early on, you may have to learn to navigate both.

*****

I started off with a small, fast-casual restaurant before expanding into catering, later adding pop-ups and eventually moving into contract meals, concessions, and product development. Potential clients would inquire about whether I had experience with contract meals or concessions and, even if I did not, the answer was always an enthusiastic, "Yes!"

It's all food to me, and it can surely be figured out with the proper amount of research and the right team. So, don't overthink or over research everything, as that is the surest way to talk yourself out of something that could prove to be worthwhile.

By doing as much research as I needed to solve a problem or acquire the information I sought, I was able to reach several milestones, including an upcoming ten-year anniversary (2026).

Just like I had to learn, know that you cannot listen to everyone. So try listening to those individuals, mentors and business owners who are doing *exactly* what you want to be doing with some degree of success and longevity. When the opportunity presents to connect with one or more of them, equip yourself with thoughtful questions so as not to waste their valuable time.

When it comes to hiring, be intentional. Try hiring the right people for the right positions. This may not apply to friends and family unless they are uniquely qualified to do the work.

Remember, it is your name on the door, the menu, and everything else. No matter who makes a mistake, what does not get done or how bad things get, it is you who will be blamed; it is your brand that will likely suffer.

Ultimately, your business is your responsibility. I'll reiterate: The buck starts and stops with you. There is little sense in ruining perfectly good friendships or family relationships to realize your dream. It is always business, never personal, but not everyone will see it that way or understand should you have to make a tough decision. So, hire accordingly. Try to bring people onboard who have integrity and who will show up. Anything else, including cooking, can be taught; character cannot.

Don't prejudge.

I hire older people, younger people, and everyone in between. I once hired a young lady, right out of high school, to cook. She had taken culinary classes from grade school through high school and was winning local cooking competitions with ease, including two that I had judged.

She sought me out after graduating, and I encouraged her to interview at several restaurants, including high-end restaurants in the downtown area to consider all of her options. After several weeks, she returned and was confident that she would get a better learning experience with me and my staff. She was right, but she had to come to that conclusion on her own.

She became highly skilled at mastering the recipes, opening and closing the restaurant, catering, managing pop-ups, and every other aspect of the business. She was mostly quiet, kept to herself, and had zero interest in supervising or managing others. She simply wanted to cook and nothing more.

After a few years, I encouraged her to consider other opportunities to expand her knowledge and experience, and she did. She left Evelyn's Food Love and went into institutional cooking and disliked it. She never said anything until I ran into her sometime later and discovered she had completely left culinary. A few months later, when an opportunity became available, I decided to gauge her interest. She accepted my offer and returned to my employ, even more mature than before and still doing an amazing job.

Had I discounted her initially because she was a teen or because she lacked experience, I would have missed out on a great employee who became a highly skilled cook and valuable member of my team. She was never late and rarely called off work. Character… You can't teach that.

As my biggest assets and a huge part of my success, I appreciate and compliment my staff often. Paying them well whenever possible encourages loyalty rather than turnover that will cause staff to leave your employ for fifty cents more to work down the street for someone else.

As important as it is to hire properly, it is equally important to part company with staff or even interns who, if despite your best efforts, simply cannot cut it. We once terminated an intern on his first day when he showed up to work with a boombox blasting music while he trained. He also brought raw food from home intending to cook it in our kitchen for his lunch. He protested loudly when the manager asked him to put the items away and that part was disruptive and unacceptable.

Also important is the ability to consistently provide great customer service. When great service becomes the norm, people can be quite forgiving of minor mishaps. Surprisingly, this can be true even if food occasionally misses the mark.

Generally, poor customer service is a deal breaker. Know that anyone can (and often will) post reviews online—even inaccurate reviews—so do try to exceed expectations. Listen to your customers and fix legitimate errors quickly and fairly. Respond to reviews—good, bad, or indifferent—directly and honestly and without being defensive. Like it or not, people are entitled to their opinions, no matter how imprecise.

I love to cook and creating something delicious from simple, raw ingredients gives me great pleasure. I also love seeing people get lost in a good meal, especially one prepared by myself or my team. There were, however, many times when a customer arrived at the restaurant angry at the world, for whatever reason, and took their anger out on my staff. They may have also been looking for a reason to write a bad review, too. After a great meal and stellar customer service, I have seen one or two customers return to the counter apologetic and with a healthy heaping of contrition.

People will always remember how you made them feel. So my staff and I try not to engage negatively just because someone else is having a bad day—one that we did not cause or in any way contribute to.

Make changes when necessary. If your "famous" pasta sauce, barbecue sauce, or whatever the recipe is, isn't moving, then update it, remix it, or nix it altogether. Do not commit to menu items that are not moving and are therefore not profitable. Conversely, if you have a secret sauce that your customers cannot get enough of, consider bottling it to create another revenue stream.

You are guaranteed to make the occasional mistake, more likely a great many mistakes as you can see I have. You might sometimes have to eat your mistakes rather than passing them, or any related costs, on to your customers. Hold your breath, chew quickly and swallow that mistake fast. Then move on and try to do better the next time.

I have miscalculated catering costs more than once. That was my fault, so I had to eat the mistake rather than passing the cost on to my client. I learned quickly, and did not make a habit of miscalculating costs. I also do not conduct business based on what someone else wants to pay. The price is the price, and it has to make good business sense as well as make money. Utilize multiple menus in multiple price points and don't haggle.

Take advantage of every free resource available to you through city, state, county, federal, or private programs and initiatives. Tap into universities that may offer small business growth cohorts with free services and programs designed to provide real-world experiences to their students while also providing your business with free consulting or other valuable services.

We had amazing experiences with the Small Business Growth Program through The Polsky Center for Entrepreneurship and Innovation at the University of Chicago. Their brilliant undergrad and graduate students, under the direction of their highly skilled business coach and program professor, assisted us with solving a couple of business-related issues we'd been grappling with. They did so effortlessly and more swiftly than we could have, given our other responsibilities at the time.

The ASCEND2020 program at Northwestern University was a four-day residential program at their Executive Center in Evanston, Illinois sponsored by Chase Bank. It was an immersive experience, exposing small business owners to a series of workshops led by a host of prominent speakers including Jim Lowry, a nationally recognized strategic advisor for Boston Consulting Group. The ASCEND2020 program is now national and offered through the University of Washington's Foster School of Business.

Loyola University's Business Law Clinic also assisted us with understanding and executing our McCormick Place contract through their law school with the help of some of their highly capable law students.

Helping others, even when resources were scarce was extremely gratifying and precisely what benefited us during the pandemic. People remember good deeds long after you have forgotten and will speak your name in important rooms even when you are not present.

Learn from your mistakes but do not dwell on them. Everyone makes mistakes and successful businesspeople understand that when you take "failure" out of the equation, you can better focus on either succeeding or learning. Use mistakes to learn, grow your business and succeed. Give yourself plenty of grace and keep moving forward. If something is not working, change it. Always, always, always pay attention to the details because details do matter.

When all else fails, bet on you. You will likely never let *you* down; you will be your greatest supporter and loudest cheerleader. Keep in mind that most culinary programs exist to teach students how to work for others, and there is absolutely nothing wrong with that. I, however, am more interested in those same students learning to eventually navigate how to successfully work for themselves. Be entrepreneurial, own their businesses and create generational wealth.

Staying motivated, prepared, focused, disciplined and resilient will aide tremendously in setting yourself up for success. You will not have to ask for a seat at someone else's table. Instead, you will position yourself to build your own table, put it in your own restaurant, and invite others to have a seat.

*****

As you can see, I spent a great deal of time working in my business until I understood every aspect of the business and could teach, train, and trust others to effectively work in the business so that I could run the entire operation – even remotely. I learned early on to give my staff the tools they needed to do a great job, and then let them. Once I was sure that was the case, I was more comfortable delegating and began working on scaling my business through other ventures.

If you simply want to cook, there is absolutely nothing wrong with that. Working for someone else is a realistic option that most of us exercise. A viable option that will allow you to enjoy doing what you love with less stress. Working for someone else will also allow you to learn and make mistakes on someone else's dime. If cooking is where your passion lies, then perhaps ownership is not for you. When you become an owner, you will likely cook less as you will also need to learn how to operate every aspect of your business. The plan, obviously, being to stay in business.

Knowing your numbers will be crucial to keeping your business open. It's okay if you are not good with numbers today, but you should get good with numbers eventually. You need to know how to determine if you are making money, doing well or need to make adjustments.

Take a class, hire someone dependable, swallow your pride, and learn what you do not know—costing menus, food cost percentages, profit margins, and the like are crucial. I did not go into great detail here because there are plenty of books on the subject. One extremely useful handbook that can help get you started is listed here and in the resources at the end titled, *Applied Math for Food Service*, by Sarah Labensky. Give it a look. I also did not go into extreme detail here because a more thorough workshop is in the works to address the finances more completely.

Finally, by all means, learn to play the long game so that you can play the game longer – and win!

Stay in touch so that I can come by your spot, see what you're up to, and celebrate what you've learned and your success! I will travel for good food!

Resources

The following is a brief list of several agencies or resources that I utilized in my quest to open Evelyn's Food Love. Please note that some of these programs may no longer exist or may only exist in the Chicagoland area. Do your research. Remember, resources found on college and university campuses can be helpful, too.

Applied Math for Food Service by Sarah R. Labensky

ASCEND/Chase Bank/ ascendcities.com

Business Affairs and Consumer Protection (BACP) / https://www.chicago.gov

Business Enterprise Program (BEP) / cei.illinois.gov

Chicago Urban League (CUL) / https:chiul.org

Choose Chicago / https://www.choosechicago.come

Government Accountability and Transparency Act (GATA) / https://gata.illinois.gov

Greater Chatham Initiative (GCI) / https://www.greaterchathaminitiative.org

Local Initiatives Support Corporation (LISC) / https://www.lisc.org

Loyola University – Business Law Clinic/School of Law / https://www.luc.edu/law/academics/clinical-programs/businesslawclinic/

Neighborhood Opportunity Fund (NOF) / https://www.chicago.gov

Polsky Center for Entrepreneurship and Innovation / https://polsky.uchicago.edu

Service Core of Retired Executives (SCORE) / https://www.score.org

Small Business Administration (SBA) / https://www.sba.gov

Small Business Improvement Fund (SBIF) / https://www.chicago.gov

System for Award Management / https://sam.gov

University of Chicago/Small Business Growth (SBG) Program

Review

Being a skilled chef with a passion for cooking does not necessarily warrant opening a restaurant. Opening a restaurant requires an "entrepreneurial mindset," and Chef Evelyn Shelton's journey thus far in her book *Carving Out a Culinary Career* exemplifies this mentality.

Chef Evelyn holds a master's degree in public administration, a bachelor's degree from Columbia College, a culinary degree, and a pastry certificate from Kendall College. She also participates in various free cohorts and learning opportunities to further her business education.

A crucial aspect of her success is understanding her financials including recipe costing, market pricing, and monitoring food and labor expenses. This financial acumen has enabled her to make informed decisions regarding business contracts. Chef Evelyn efficiently manages her time, ensuring she dedicates sufficient time to working "*on*" her business rather than solely "*in*" her business, which she achieves by building and leveraging a great team.

Diversification of revenue streams has been another key strategy for Chef Evelyn. Beyond relying on her storefront, she engages in various ventures such as meal programs, operations at the McCormick Place Convention Center, pop-ups, concessions and consumer packaged goods (CPG).

These endeavors, combined with her extensive network of contacts, have significantly increased awareness of her offerings and capabilities, leading to numerous interviews, articles, and other media appearances.

Additionally, Chef Evelyn has effectively secured capital grants, overcoming the typical "access to capital" challenges that frequently impede small, minority-owned businesses, thereby enabling her to expand her restaurant.

Chef Evelyn's experiences and strategies serve as a master class in small business entrepreneurship providing invaluable lessons and should be considered essential reading for food entrepreneurs at any stage of their careers.

John Handler, Industrial Cluster Manager, Greater Chatham Initiative, Chicago

About the Author

Chef Evelyn, as she is popularly known, is the chef/owner of Evelyn's Food Love in Chicago where she currently resides. She honed her business and culinary skills as an Executive Chef with the Morrison Division of Compass Group.

Chef Evelyn is a graduate of Kendall College, the top culinary school in the region, where she completed an accelerated culinary arts program while excelling in Kendall's baking and pastry arts program simultaneously. Well-rounded, she also holds a bachelor's degree from Columbia College and a master's degree from Roosevelt University. So impressed with their alum, Chef Evelyn received the "Social Justice Award" from Roosevelt in 2021 for her work in the community...a nice companion piece to the NAACP ACT-SO award she received previously.

Chef Evelyn and her culinary creations have been featured on: ABC 7's "The Hungry Hound with Steve Dolinsky," Windy City Live, The Black Foodies, Chicago Tonight on WTTW, in The Chicago Sun-Times, Patch Chicago, Black Chicago Eats, Eater Chicago, LISC Chicago, The Chicago Defender, Chicago Woman Magazine, Black Food and Beverage (blackfandb), on WVON Radio, WBBM Radio, WGN Radio, "Operation Breadbasket presents Harambee" Radio, Heritage Radio's "A Hungry Society," Crain's Chicago Business, Forbes.com, Afros and Knives as well as by the Chicago Reader in "The Iconic Chicago Restaurants" issue. She has also been featured in James Beard Foundation's Beard Bites.

Chef Evelyn is a widely sought after and featured guest, contributor and panelist by media outlets and various community organizations discussing many topics, including minority businesses and the importance of community development, equity and inclusion. She is currently penning her first cookbook while working on bringing her spices, sauces, and other fare to the marketplace. One of her major goals is to develop a culinary training program on the south side of Chicago to help provide employment opportunities in these often overlooked and under-resourced communities.

Construction of the new rooftop bar addition to her restaurant is scheduled to begin in early 2026.

Join the Conversation

Follow Chef Evelyn Shelton on social media for updates, inspiration, and sneak peeks into the world of *Carving Out a Culinary Career*. Aspiring entrepreneurs and fans of culinary storytelling won't want to miss the chance to journey through the pages of this remarkable book.

Don't miss the opportunity to uncover the secrets of success in the restaurant business. *Carving Out a Culinary Career* is your ultimate insight into navigating the highs and lows of culinary entrepreneurship.

www.evelynsfoodlove.com

Follow me on social media:
Instagram: @evelynsfoodlove_
Facebook: evelynsfoodlove5522

www.ingramcontent.com/pod-product-compliance
Lightning Source LLC
Chambersburg PA
CBHW050911160426
43194CB00011B/2363